HERON HILL CHRONICLE

BOOKS BY GEORGE REIGER

Zane Grey: Outdoorsman

Profiles in Saltwater Angling

Fishing with McClane

The Zane Grey Cookbook (co-author)

The Audubon Society Book of Marine Wildlife

The Wings of Dawn

The Undiscovered Zane Grey Fishing Stories

Wanderer on My Native Shore

Southeast Coast

Floaters and Stick-Ups

The Birder's Journal

The Wildfowler's Quest

The Silver King

The Bonefish

Heron Hill Chronicle

Heron Hill
Chronicle

George Reiger

 Lyons & Burford, Publishers

Printed in the United States of America

Design by Cindy LaBreacht

10 9 8 7 6 5 4 3 2 1

ALL LINE ART BY GORDON ALLEN

Library of Congress Cataloging-in-Publication Data
Reiger, George, 1939–
    Heron Hill Chronicle / George Reiger.
        p.   cm.
    ISBN 1-55821-296-5 (cloth)
    1. Reiger, George, 1939– . 2. Outdoor writers—United States—
Biography. 3. Heron Hill (Va.) I. Title.
SK 17.R45A3 1994
639.9'09755' 16—dc20
                                                94-22675
                                                CIP

CONTENTS

Here nature and liberty afford us that freely which in England we want, or it costeth us dearly.... [There are no] hard landlords to rack us with high rents, or extorting fines... [no] tedious pleas in law to consume us with their many years' disputation for justice.... Here every man may be master of his own labor and land.

—CAPTAIN JOHN SMITH'S DESCRIPTION OF VIRGINIA, 1624

Indians, Europeans & African emigrants, & their descendents have been living on this rise of ground between two streams & the salt marsh for hundreds of years. In all those centuries, nothing significant has happened here. We trust you will respect our wishes to keep things that way, for only young men & fools desire to live through "interesting" times.

—THE AUTHOR'S ENTRANCE SIGN TO HERON HILL, 1974

MARYLAND

Chesapeake Bay

DELAWARE

VIRGINIA

MD.

VA.

Heron Hill

Atlantic Ocean

C. REIGER
1991

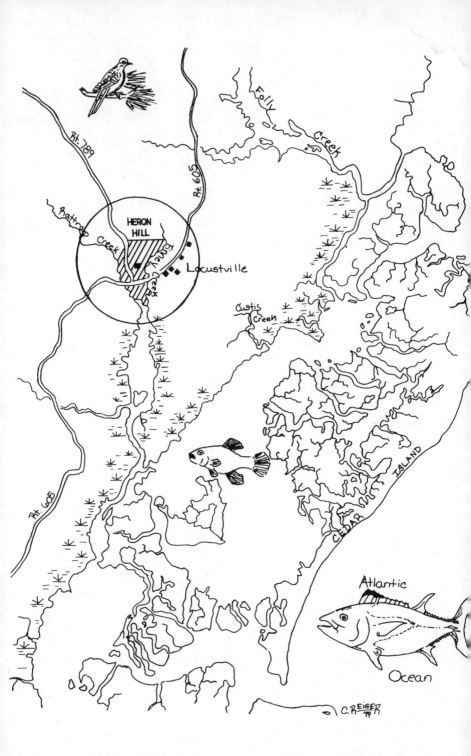

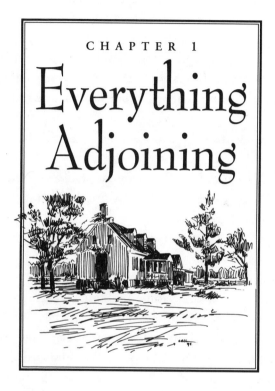

CHAPTER 1

Everything Adjoining

B efore we bought the farm, Barbara and I didn't know what we wanted exactly—much less what we could afford. I knew little about small-building construction and less about farming. I wasn't even sure what a dormer is, and had I been, I wouldn't have imagined that I would end up living in a house with ten of them.

There were just three real estate offices on the Eastern Shore of Virginia in 1970. (Today, there are more than twenty.) Two of the three had sent their most ambitious salespeople to seminars where they'd learned that a good agent shows a prospective client only a few properties that suit the client's profile. At the time, Barbara and I were categorized as "young married professionals." Seminar-wise salespeople, therefore, insisted that we were looking for a waterfront lot near the country club. We said that if we'd wanted such a property, we could have found one a lot closer to New York City. The seminar grads persisted, however, figuring that if we didn't like Subdivision A, we'd go for Subdivision B.

By contrast, C. J. Prettyman & Son were so low-key we met the son, Bill, only once, and C. J. not at all. Better yet, they never called us; we called them. They had an empty office in an otherwise vacant building in Exmore where mimeographed flyers of available properties were kept under random-size fishing weights so they wouldn't blow away if someone opened the door. Bill admitted that not every flyer represented a property for sale. Some listings were by people curious to know what their fallback positions would be if they couldn't make a crop that year. Bill told us that if a particular property intrigued us, he'd let us know whether it was a serious offering or just a "market tester." If a serious offering, he'd either have his assistant, Wayne Fincen, a retired state trooper, meet us or, if Wayne had a prior commitment—on Saturdays he was often busy with his kids' ball games—tell us how to find the property on our own and where its key, if any, was kept.

Although Barbara and I made two honeymoon trips that spring—one to the Virgin Islands and another on a houseboat up the Arkansas River—those trips were magazine assignments and hence, work. Our weekend dashes to Virginia—where we stayed for $8 a night in the Whispering Pines Motel and poked around the back roads of Accomack and Northampton Counties—were our real honeymoon, albeit one enjoyed in bimonthly installments.

Barbara's colleagues at Doubleday and mine at Hearst were baffled or amused when we began looking for property south of the Mason-Dixon line. New Yorkers who thought nothing of driving five or six hours to weekend retreats in New England asked us how we could make the same length trip "down there." What they were really asking was how we could contemplate buying property in what they considered to be the Third World. Even though these friends shared our wavelengths in other respects, they forgot that, although Barbara's mother was in the New York Social Register, her father was from Savannah, where Barbara was born and brought up; and although my father, like me, had been born in Brooklyn, my mother was born and reared in Halifax County, Virginia. The South was not an alien culture to either Barbara or me.

We had shared many weekends on the Eastern Shore before, after, and in between my navy tours in Vietnam: while I was in language school in Washington and Barbara visited from Atlanta, when I was teaching at the Naval Academy and Barbara was based in Washington with an airline, and before I left Annapolis for the Paris Peace Talks and Barbara worked for an Alabama Congressman. We started our search for a home near Ocean City, Maryland, but found it crowded and changed from the little fishing village I remembered aboard my father's boat just after World War II, so we bent south on Route 13 and eventually found the time warp we were seeking in Accomack County.*

I longed for land, and Barbara yearned to restore an old house. I would have settled for living in a trailer so long as it was surrounded by as much land as I could buy with the money the trailer saved me. Marriage, however, modifies a man's priorities. Barbara's desire for a traditional home became mine as well, so we offered more than we could afford for a partially renovated mansion with its own guest house on several acres of land overlooking Nassawadox Creek. The asking price was $77,000, and Wayne thought it unlikely that the owner would take less than $72,000. Still, we went ahead and bid $67,000. As Wayne drove us back to the motel, wandering from bayside to seaside, he casually pointed to a traditional Eastern Shore telescoping house overlooking the marsh just west of Locustville and said that it was for sale.

"Stop!" Barbara and I said in unison.

We sat in Wayne's car while he warned us that the owner was a peculiar duck who wouldn't negotiate his price.

"How much does he want?" Barbara asked.

"Twenty-five thousand."

---

* The county is spelled Accomack—with a *k*; the county seat is spelled Accomac—without. This was done a century ago to make it easier to distinguish the town from the county in legal documents.

We gasped.

"How much land?" I asked.

"Sixty-seven acres," said Wayne. I gasped again. "Only about twenty-two acres are cultivated, though. The rest is marsh and woods with, maybe, some decent pine."

"When can we see it?"

The next morning it was Wayne's turn to be astonished when Barbara and I cheered and danced after he told us that our bid on the Nassawadox property had been rejected. We told him to offer the Locustville owner what he wanted. When Wayne still looked perplexed, I explained that since we'd just "saved" $67,000 by not buying the Nassawadox property, we could easily afford the Locustville farm. Barbara and I had calculated that with our combined incomes of nearly $25,000, we'd be able to meet both a farm mortgage and an apartment rent in Manhattan. Of course, we hadn't yet learned that restoration generates its own financial black hole. Nor had I yet become obsessed with acquiring four supplemental properties that were part of the original plat when the farm was carved out of coastal wilderness in the early 1700s.

Wayne served as our agent for the first of these acquisitions. The eight-acre lot cost nearly $4,000, but that was because it included a large Victorian house and outbuilding. When I tried to explain my plan to Wayne, he said he understood: "You don't want it all. You just want everything adjoining."

CHAPTER 2

Restlessness

Moving is like murder: Done once, it becomes easier the second and subsequent times around. Unlike our European cousins, who—if wars permit—are content to live in the same towns that their great-grandparents built, Americans move on and build new nests as soon as the old foraging grounds are exhausted—more like our primate relatives. In 1835, Alexis de Tocqueville observed that "in the United States, a man builds a house in which to spend his old age, and he sells it before the roof is on."

My wife and I are typical offspring of this restless culture. If I count boarding school, college, graduate schools and navy postings of more than six months, I'd lived in two dozen places by the time Barbara and I were married. She'd lived in an even dozen, which, according to the U.S. Bureau of Census, is the precise average for every American during his or her lifetime. No wonder so many old friends marvel that Barbara and I have now been living in the same village with fewer than a hundred registered voters for more than two decades. Yet once we were gone from New York and Washington, we never looked back. We not only didn't sell the house before the roof was on, we recently replaced half its asphalt shingles with cedar shakes. It's the fifth such roof in the 240-year history of the east wing.

The irony of our culture's cavalier attitude toward continuity is that in our hearts, we know it's wrong. By constantly moving—generally to a higher plateau of debt—we bequeath to those who follow many of the unpalatable ingredients of our former lives. We also set an example for the entire world. Elsewhere, moving was once a matter of necessity. Increasingly, however, other societies move in the hope of parlaying sufficiency into luxury. Ironically, America's dispossessed are the only class that can't move; they don't have enough money.

Still, in our national holidays, we pay homage to the myth of permanence. From Fourth of July parades down Main Street to Thanksgiving dinner at Grandma's,

Americans worship the ideals of rural rootedness. Countless men and women endure decades of corporate indenture in the expectation that one day they'll be able to break out and buy "a place in the country." The longer they wait, however, the more unlikely the dream becomes, and not merely because land keeps getting more expensive. Rural newcomers who've spent their formative years in and around cities have trouble adjusting to small communities, where money is less important than relationships, and where time is measured in seasons, not seconds. American urbanites are as bewildered as Oscar Wilde, who noted that "people in the country get up early, because there's so much to do. They go to bed early, because there's nothing to talk about." Others agree with Henry David Thoreau that "we soon get through with Nature; she excites an expectation which she cannot satisfy."

City people work and play by the hour and are willing to postpone present opportunities for future rewards. Country people, by contrast, track time by the turning of the earth. They seize each day because a missed morning of farming or fishing may mean a missed season, and a missed season may mean bankruptcy. Alternate-side-of-the-street parking rules make perfect sense in a city, but let a resource administrator propose a regulation prohibiting fishermen from working certain days of the week, and all hell breaks loose. People who earn their livings from the sea work when the wind and the moon (the tides) permit them to work, not when some calendar-conscious bureaucrat says they can.

Corporate executives seem to have the greatest difficulty adjusting to rural life. One of the half-dozen *Field & Stream* publishers I've known during two decades of writing for the magazine once asked what I did on the farm for amusement.

"How do you mean?" I asked. "The farm is my amusement."

"Well, what do you do at night?" asked Mike O'Neill.

"Same as you: read, watch TV, go to bed."

"On weekends?"

"Weekends and weekdays are the same, except that I avoid weekend fishing to avoid the crowds. I try to write something every morning and be outdoors every afternoon. For that reason, dove and deer hunting and bass fishing fit into my schedule better than duck hunting or offshore fishing, which generally means an entire day lost from writing."

"Sounds nice," said Mike. "But I'd go nuts!"

When we began restoring the house, Barbara and I drove up to Salisbury, Maryland, to order large, handmade bricks for the chimneys. The clerk asked where to deliver them.

"Locustville, Virginia," I replied.

"Where's that?" he asked.

"Between Accomac and Wachapreague."

The clerk started to write, then paused to say with both wonder and scorn, "It's like 1940 down there."

It's more like 1960 today, but our neighbors and we are still thankfully behind the times in many respects. Few of us lock our doors during the day. At night, with an east wind blowing, we hear the ocean booming on the desert-ed beach beyond the marsh. Many people imagine that they'd love to live here, but few are able to make the leap and stay.

The retired couple from whom we bought the core of our now 260-acre farm had been too devoted to external authority to remain on the Shore. He was a retired army colonel who liked to lecture local workmen on the virtues of promptness and good posture. He had hoped to estab-lish a nursery by planting azaleas, magnolias, and camellias under the pines out back and apple, cherry, and peach trees in the open ground between the chicken house and the well. He had hoped that the nursery would eventually sup-port itself with a minimum of maintenance. The flowering shrubs did well, but the apples were always blemished, the cherries got pecked by the birds, and the peach trees fought a losing battle against borers and blight.

The colonel's wife had been raised in Berlin (Germany, not Maryland) and put a little extra spin on her delivery with anyone who was less cosmopolitan than herself—which meant just about everyone around here. She was imbued with the Nordic ideal of sampling equal parts of nature and culture. The problem is that the two tend to be mutually exclusive in America. The couple's only child spent most of his time playing war games with his father in a sandpile in the front yard while his mother sat on the porch and muttered about the once and future glories of Deutschland.

Not long after acquiring the farm, the colonel began testing its resale value. By the time Barbara and I came along and agreed to give him twice what he'd originally paid, he took our money and ran. Fifteen years later, his son returned to see what we'd done to the place. The colonel had died in the meantime and the boy's mother had remarried. The young man obviously missed his dad, so I didn't have the heart to present him with all the plastic soldiers I'd found in the sandpile and been saving for his return.

Truth and wisdom tend to be as mutually exclusive in our society as culture and nature. When I worked in New York and Washington, my information-oriented colleagues and I believed that facts were the essential building blocks of truth and justice. As I get older, however, I understand that truth is much more elusive than I previously imagined, and its pursuit may distract from the larger goal of wisdom. Like "interesting times," truth is something that intrigues mostly the young. As we age, we gradually realize it's knowledge that matters, and knowledge can come only with the regular performance of a useful skill. Planting and tending crops and slaughtering one's own food are not familiar tasks for most people, yet they're routine rituals for me and many of my neighbors. It's practice that makes perfection of self-reliance, and it's self-reliance that provides the only access to wisdom. Academic credentials and corporate titles only get in the way.

CHAPTER 3

The Cemetery

I t's surprising how few of our visitors notice the cemetery. Some weekend guests come and go without seeing the graveyard and subsequently think that I'm putting them on when I mention it. Other are more observant. Film producer Dale Bell rushed into our house on a Sunday morning to inform the other guests: "The Reigers have people buried in their front yard!"

I sometimes spur interest in the cemetery by announc-
ing that Audubon and Stonewall Jackson are buried there.
Most people think I'm joking, but a few imagine that it's
possible—that through some quirk of history, John James
Audubon and Thomas "Stonewall" Jackson did end up in
our front yard. In both cases, however, they forget that
many children were named for cultural heroes. Our
Stonewall Jackson's family name was Kellam, and he was
only four months and twenty-four days old when he died
on October 3, 1868. The Civil War had been over for only
a few years, and many Virginians still believed that had
General Jackson not been mortally wounded at
Chancellorsville, the rebellion might have had a different
ending.

Audubon Kellam's given name is more surprising.
Although John James Audubon was lionized in Baltimore
salons, he was less well known in the farming communities
of the Eastern Shore. Yet the connection is unmistakable:
John James Audubon died in 1851, and the infant
Audubon Kellam died the following year.

Cultural historians rarely consider how a high death
rate among children influenced our ancestors' values. Any
American born since the mid-twentieth century takes for
granted such industrial marvels as screen windows and
antiviral medicines. We don't often reflect on the countless
lives saved by preventing disease-bearing insects from
reaching potential victims or by treating children for infec-
tions that would otherwise have killed them. As recently as
my mother's generation, childhood mortality rates were
very high. She and her brother and sister were the only

three of their parents' eight offspring to survive childhood. In cemeteries around South Boston, Virginia, half the headstones commemorating members of the Dance family are for those who never reached puberty, just as half the headstones in our Locustville graveyard are for Ashbys, Bloxoms, and Kellams who were infants or children when they died. The tallest monument in the graveyard, whose pinnacle is toppled each year by the heaving of frost and subsequent thaw, commemorates a brother and sister who died within a week of each other in 1892. The girl was four and a half years old; her brother, only twenty-two months.

In cool weather, or when biting insects are kept at bay by a brisk ocean breeze, I sometimes take guests on a brief tour of the cemetery. It's well shaded by hackberries, planted by birds that pass the seeds while perched on the marble markers. Appropriately enough, one of the largest hackberry trees thrusts up from Audubon Kellam's grave, and its trunk and roots are gradually growing over the headstone's inscription. Between the markers, surviving members of the family planted several now-antique varieties of daffodils.

Although the oldest headstones belong to James Ashby (1767–1837) and his sequential wives, the most impressive are large neo-Gothic markers from the late Victorian era with elaborately carved designs: the Masonic emblem on the stone of John R. Kellam, the rose for his wife, and the sleeping lambs for their children who predeceased them. "King John," as this patriarch was known (and not always affectionately), made a substantial living in the usual way most affluent people in the farming or fishing business do:

by processing rather than producing. In Kellam's case, this meant operating the gristmill on Rattrap Creek. Kellam was the only miller for miles around, and he was reputed to have been rather ruthless when it came to protecting his monopoly. A relative once remarked, "If I thought that Cousin John had a chance of going to heaven, I'd start applying now for the other place."

Margaret Walker, who grew up in Locustville, remembers the shy thrill she felt as a little girl at the turn of the century, wending her way through the bustle of men, mules and wagons on the sandy road outside the mill. John Kellam died in 1890, but a shrewd idea he introduced was kept in practice until shipping rates on the New York, Philadelphia, and Norfolk Railroad[*] made it more profitable for farmers to sell their grain off the Shore and import their flour. Each of King John's regular customers had a jug with his name glazed on it sitting on a shelf in a breezeway known as the Chapel. The jug contained liquor distilled from whatever grain the farmer preferred. While a customer waited for his wagon to be loaded with sacks of flour exchanged for the grain he'd brought to the mill, he'd "meditate" in the Chapel. Sometimes "worshippers" would stay long after their wagons were loaded. They later grumbled that Kellam's exchange rate favored King John, yet they had no one to blame but themselves and their personalized jugs.

---

* The "Nip 'n N" was bought and expanded by the Pennsylvania Railroad Company in 1908.

I usually end my cemetery tour by the front stoop, where I point to the broken millstone that Barbara and I found one Sunday afternoon while probing with a metal rod at the old mill site. Now bordered by brick and embedded in concrete, the wedge of millstone may be a more lasting tribute to John R. Kellam than his headstone, whose lettering has eroded significantly even during our brief tenure as custodians. Other stones, especially those that lean back to the sky, have become illegible in the quarter century we've been here, and one cut from inferior marble is actually dissolving like a slab of sugar. The disintegration of these grave markers is more redolent of memento mori than any inscription to the effect: "As you are now, I once was too." The dilemma is whether to spend money trying to save the stones or to accept the inevitable. I've epoxy-repaired two of the broken markers and regularly re-erect those that fall over. Each spring, Barbara cuts back encroaching weeds. But short of bringing the stones indoors or putting a canopy over the entire cemetery to protect it from acidified rain, there's no way to save marble from the passage of time.

Besides, a grave marker is just that. It helps perpetuate the memory of an individual for his or her family and friends as long as they're alive. Once the last of those who personally knew the deceased is gone, the marker may evoke a generalized melancholy, but no more so than does an abandoned house or a tractor overgrown with weeds. Still, to remove a headstone is to desecrate a grave more completely than exhuming its remains. When you dig up the dead, you dishonor them. But when you remove a gravestone, you annihilate memory.

When Barbara and I first came here, there was still a seventeenth-century graveyard on a neck not far south whose slate headstones looked from a distance as though angels were carved into them. When you got close, however, you saw that the designs were actually human skulls with wings. Over the past two decades, the farmer who worked that property plowed, disked, and planted in ever-diminishing circles around the graveyard. Every few years, his machinery knocked over another stone and scattered the broken pieces. When only a few whole stones were left, they disappeared—perhaps into someone's care. Today, you can no longer tell where the graveyard was. An anonymous field of grain grows where the markers once stood. Ironically, slate withstands acidic precipitation better than marble, and most of the slate stones cut in the 1600s were more legible than the 1800s marble markers in our front yard. The pity and crime are that the seventeenth-century graveyard was obliterated not by time but before its time, by human indifference.

It's neither the age of our cemetery nor the names of the people buried here (unless visitors share the same last names) that intrigue most guests. It's the cemetery itself, just fifty yards from our front stoop. City visitors are surprised that people back then didn't bury their dead in a churchyard or some other communal ground out of sight—and out of mind—of surviving relatives. Landless people, of course, did and still do that. In the nineteenth century, however, Sundays were regularly devoted to contemplating the inevitability of death, putting fresh flowers on the graves of relatives, and even picnicking in the cemetery where you planned to spend eternity.

Our ancestors liked having their deceased kith and kin nearby. So do the majority of people on earth. The most ignorant aspect of our government's peasant resettlement policy during the Vietnam War was that we separated families, and even entire villages, from their ancestral burial grounds. Who would look after the graves of grandfathers once their children were sent to "governmentally secure areas" far away? How dare Americans put their political interests ahead of the moral obligations of the Vietnamese to maintain their ancestral links?

About once a year, Barbara and I have visitors who come specifically to see the cemetery. Some use topographical maps to locate it and ask our permission to make charcoal rubbings of the gravestones. Others come to see the graves of ancestors. The rubbers are generally more cordial, because they appear to appreciate what Barbara and I have done to maintain the stones; the relatives sometimes suggest that we haven't done enough. One woman remarked that the rain which drove us back to the house that morning must be the reason for the weeds around the tombstones. Another thought we had no right to remove the fence that once surrounded the graveyard, but doing so has made it easier to control the weeds.

Without anyone else to look after them, the Ashbys, Bloxoms, and Kellams who are buried here have become ancestors by proxy. And just as in other instances of adoption, the history of the people buried here has become part of our own heritage. We not only live in the same house they lived in, farm the same fields, and explore the same woods but also know more of the day-to-day details of their lives than we do of the activities of our own great-grandparents.

I like to imagine that our interest and empathy are what finally laid to rest the ghost that used to haunt the living room. On the floor beneath the rug is an old bloodstain that not even our most vigorous scouring could remove. I don't know whether that bloodstain is linked to the mysterious opening and closing of the living-room door or the murmuring voices we occasionally heard while lying in bed upstairs, but the last of these inexplicable events occurred over a decade ago. Of course, that was about the time we screened over the living-room chimney to prevent swifts from nesting there. We did leave the huge kitchen chimney unscreened, and every year we welcome the birds' return from Peru. Their chattering sometimes sounds like murmuring voices, but so far the swifts have been unable to open or close the living-room door.

CHAPTER 4

My Own Labor and Land

I'm sometimes asked how—born in Brooklyn, reared in Queens, and with my fast-track choice of more conventional careers—I could drop out of the race and find bliss as a freelance writer on a farm in coastal Virginia. Part of the answer is provided by the man who built the fence in our lower yard. He had been pressed by many other job offers that spring, so why had he come to work here instead of somewhere else? Gesturing toward the marsh and the bay beyond, he replied, "I don't work no place I can't see water."

A larger answer has to do with my upbringing. At the age of ten, I was sent to Lawrenceville, at the time an all-boys' boarding school. I was one of fifteen students in an experimental, and now thankfully defunct, seventh grade known as the Shell Form. The touted reason for our being there was that we were wunderkinder. The real reason was that we were from dysfunctional but well-heeled families whose parents thought that boarding school would be best for us.

To sustain the wunderkind myth, Lawrenceville assigned some of its best-credentialed faculty to teach us. Master's degrees and Ph.D.s, however, mean little to youngsters who are yearning for role models, and few of our superiorly educated teachers spent any time with us outside of class. Our dormitory masters were equally reluctant to spend more than the minimum time required. Our real education, therefore, took place at night, when the student bullies and quislings—many of whom have since made brilliant careers in business and politics—ran protection rackets, organized raids on other houses, and persecuted anyone who just wanted to be left alone. By the end of my first year, one classmate had committed suicide, another had suffered a nervous breakdown, and two had run away (one successfully, since his father—a diplomat—sent the boy home to Iran, where he is now a leader in the Islamic fundamentalist movement). Although nine of us survived

six years to graduate, we were all pretty much damaged
goods. Since then, another has committed suicide, and
David Decker, a day student who got to go home every
night and was, therefore, nearly normal, was killed in
Vietnam, along with much else that was once considered
normal.

My survival strategy was to spend as much time away
from the dorm as possible. My first year's hideouts included the chapel, the library, and the woods on the other side
of the school pond. (This latter sanctuary has since been
cut down for more playing fields.) One afternoon, Mr.
Keller, the choirmaster, found me doing homework in the
chapel. He said nothing, but the next time I sneaked in the
side door, I found a lamp and an extension cord there. Five
years later, I took Mr. Keller's music-appreciation course,
scored a perfect one hundred, and won the school music
prize. My effort was partly to please a teacher who had seen
a ten-year-old's unhappiness but hadn't humiliated him by
trying to intervene.

The head librarian, Mr. Thurber, was also concerned
about a new boy's reluctance to leave the library at night.
When he saw that I was interested in nature, he introduced
me to the stories of Charles G. D. Roberts; and when I
won the Shell Form short-story contest, he provided an
illustrated two-volume set of Kipling's *Jungle Books* for the
prize. He told me of another Lawrentian who'd recently
made a name for himself in "nature studies" and suggested
that I read *A Sand County Almanac.* That spring, when I
found my first Indian arrowhead in a freshly plowed field
just beyond the school grounds, I wondered whether Aldo

Leopold '05 had ever found one of his own while tramping across those same fields.

Although my best grades were in English, my favorite Shell Form course was science. In the autumn, we studied botany with Dr. Diehl. Much of what we learned was by rote and soon forgotten, but Dr. Diehl taught us how to use a scientific key and to remember that it's not what we know that matters, but how to find out. At the time, taxonomic keys were tedious to use, but a botanist named Richard Old has recently designed a computer program for plant identification that seems to be far more layperson-friendly. Instead of worrying about whether the leaves of an unknown plant are "pinnate" or its flowers have "clustered heads," the new key concerns itself with such generalities as height, habitat, color, and even whether the plant "smells bad" or "feels squishy."

Dr. Diehl also taught us an abiding respect for the oak —sixty-eight species of *Quercus* in North America alone. Years later, when Princeton's Professor George Rowley asked each of his students to draw a particular bud as it emerged in the spring to gain some insight into the philosophy of Chinese art,[*] I chose the swamp chestnut oak because its acorns are sweet enough to be eaten from the ground, because the disjunct between the early and late wood inside each growth ring is so sharp that this oak provides the best basket splints, but mostly because it thrives in wet, rich soil the way I do.

---

[*] When American children are asked to draw a tree, they generally draw a lollipop. When Asian children are asked to draw a tree, they usually draw a trunk, branches, and a few emblematic leaves.

When the weather turned slushy, the Shell Form science class moved indoors to Dr. Taylor's laboratory where this modern Merlin delighted us with sound-and-light shows he called "experiments." But since we all knew what to expect, there seemed to be nothing experimental about them. They were magic, pure and simple, and I still feel that way whenever I watch demonstrations of a vacuum, gravity, osmosis, or the explosive potential of hydrogen once it's extracted from water.

Spring term was my favorite. I enjoyed it as much for its lengthening days and the realization that I might actually survive the Shell Form as for the study of insects with Mr. _____. Like a birder who looks down on game species because they're so well known and popular, I disdained large moths and butterflies because they were the only insects that impressed my classmates. My passion was wasps and beetles. I admired the sinister aerodynamics of the one and the stubborn strength of the other.

Collecting insects, however, led to my first experience with injustice. A favorite collecting site was the weedy (not woody) side of the stream that ran into the school pond. I caught my first "big game" there—a mating pair of cicada killers—and one afternoon, I found an extraordinarily beautiful and apparently rare species of long-horned beetle (family Cerambycidae). When Mr. _____ saw it mounted in my display case, he told me that he wanted it for the school collection. Since the school didn't have a collection, I knew that Mr. _____ wanted the insect for himself. I refused—until he made clear that a crucial part of my final grade would be "cooperation." I've distrusted the word ever since.

Four years later, my faith in authority was dealt an even greater blow, but this time I softened its impact with guile. From First Form on, I ran a trapline that taught me more about nature than anything else I've ever done. Each winter morning, I got up ninety minutes before the wake-up bell; checked and relocated my traps along the golf-course and school-pond streams; skinned what I'd caught and stretched the hides; ate a quick breakfast provided by the kitchen staff, to whom I gave the muskrat and occasional raccoon carcasses; and still made compulsory chapel by 8 A.M.

In January of my Fourth Form year, I had more than a hundred skins curing in the cellar of Kennedy House. One of the kitchen staff told the housemaster about the cellar cache, and another kitchen helper warned me. I got to the cellar stairs too late to head off Dr. Chivers but in time to rescue him from his own imagination. He'd found the gloomy annex where the skins were hung on a clothesline running back and forth across the low-ceilinged room. "Bats!" he yelled, while flailing about to keep the sinister shadows at bay. "Bats! Bats!" he kept shouting. Hitting a few, he set many in motion and was still white with fear when I showed him that the "bats" were actually muskrat skins.

Upstairs, I showed him my state hunting and trapping license and argued there was nothing against trapping in school regulations. Since my grades were good, I suggested there was no reason to inform the headmaster. I feared what the headmaster would do, because two years earlier, I'd been caught by the proctor hunting rats and popping lightbulbs in the school dump with a slingshot. The head-master had confiscated my slingshot, sternly lectured me, given me five demerits, and summarized me at one of his Sunday afternoon teas as "antisocial."

I feared the worst, and I was right. The headmaster put me on report for eight weeks, gave me ten demerits at a time when fifteen would get a student expelled, and confiscated my furs so that they could be sold and the money given to the school camp fund. I could endure the demerits and the time on report—which meant that for eight weeks, the campus was a kind of low-security prison. But I could neither endure nor forgive the headmaster's expropriation of my furs. Muskrat skins were worth about a dollar each in 1954. I had been planning to buy a shot-gun and binoculars with what I earned. The headmaster's purloining of my labor and potential profit was like acid thrown on my fifteen-year-old soul.

Fortunately, no one in the school hierarchy knew how to sell raw fur, so the skins were returned to me for mar-keting. I sent them in two packages—one very large and one rather small—to two different fur houses in Manhattan. I subsequently donated the smaller of the two checks to the school camp fund. I expected some question about the modest amount and had prepared a story about how the furs had been improperly stored and had to be sold at a reduced price. But just as no one knew where to sell the furs, no one knew their value. From that time on, however, I determined that someday I'd live someplace where I could be master of my own labor and land.

CHAPTER 5

The Marsh

We've all heard that birds, upon hatching, presume that the first moving object they see is a parent and immediately form a dependency fixation which biologists call imprinting—whether that object is actually the parent, a human face, or a swinging pocket watch. The entire reproductive strategy of cowbirds is based on imprinting,

37

and many other female birds frequently lay their eggs in the nests of unrelated species. On the prairies, for example, redhead ducks may lay up to three-quarters of their eggs in the nests of other waterfowl; as much as half of this species' total reproduction may be from such eggs. In Accomack County, the state waterfowl biologist and I once monitored a nesting box in which a woodduck hen hatched four woodduck and three hooded merganser eggs. We don't know how the blended brood fared, but successful fledglings of similar combinations occur regularly.

The point is that imprinting works both ways: Parents are as taken with their offspring, no matter how unlikely, as newly hatched birds are taken with their parents, no matter how absurd. Imprinting affects every species that is dependent on one or both parents after birth. Since that includes humans, and since most humans resist any insinuation that we're like other animals, imprinting is the butt of many popular jokes. A friend of mine once reasoned that since my father was out fishing the day I was born and my mother was under a total anesthetic, and since the only significant event of the day—April 7, 1939—was Mussolini's invasion of Albania, that's the reason I love pasta. If we enlarge on my friend's silliness, we might conclude that Mussolini's unconventional life explains why I've fire-walked in Tahiti, gone swimming in the Panama Canal, been blown up in Saigon, hauled crab pots in the Orkney Islands, shot ducks in the Soviet Union, battled tuna off South Africa, and caught poisonous sea snakes in Fiji. My intellectual life has been equally unorthodox. Although my master's thesis at Columbia documented the medieval ingredients of English Renaissance theater, I taught Oliver North the rudiments of Vietnamese and tutored Lawrence E. Walsh in the history of Southeast Asian communism. But since these names may be unfamiliar to some readers, let's return to imprinting.

I was born not far from Jamaica Bay. Whether that—or another—was the first salt marsh I saw, the experience left me with an abiding love of the gold and emerald hues of cordgrass. The rocky coasts of the north Atlantic may be more spectacular, but my soul pulses with the movement of tides soughing over sod islands and muddy shores. Profound beauty can cause men pain, and my heart aches whenever I see sunlight reflected from a flooding marsh.

When we bought the farm, Barbara and I were initially quite protective of the marsh we'd purchased with it. When I saw a boy stalking blackbirds there with a .22, I charged out the front door to holler him off before remembering another boy who'd taken many steps toward his own awareness of nature with a rifle in his hands. I stood on the causeway and watched film clips of my youth. The boy missed. So, often, had I. The boy saw me and, embarrassed, left the marsh by another direction. So, sometimes, had I.

For the first few years, whenever we found time to wander, Barbara, our guests, and I launched my trailered boat and fished, clammed, or shot ducks out beyond the public ramps rather than explore the quarter mile of marsh stretching across the road. We didn't want to mar it with our footprints, although we noticed trails left by muskrats, otters, raccoons, and foxes. We believed, however, that they belonged and we didn't.

After storm tides, we even carried gunnysacks across the way to collect cans and bottles that had drifted up under the cedars. We once discovered a mahogany pallet probably dumped off a ship running up the coast from Latin America. Although the wood wasn't furniture grade, it was more than adequate to reinforce the walls of a two-seater outhouse we converted into a storage shed.

In all, we kept five of the six outbuildings that came with all the parcels of land we purchased. (The sixth shed was carted away by friends and restored on their farm.) Harness-racer and house-mover Norman West put the structures on travois and dragged them across the fields. He charged between $25 and $90, according to the size of the shed, the distance moved, and the year he did the work. We put the sheds in a row behind the main house, where they quickly filled with tools, curiosities, and junk. Nature does, indeed, loathe a vacuum.

Meanwhile, I was learning more about the marsh—and myself. Although I still felt protective, I became more tolerant of human activity as I learned the marsh's history. Decaying cedar fence posts are mute reminders of when horses, cattle, and sheep grazed there. Even as recently as the 1950s, watermen lived in oyster shacks beyond the estuary—rude affairs on pilings from which the men tended their oyster "rocks," collected clams for a penny apiece, and hunted ducks in and out of season. Today the estuary is used by the Wachapreague charter fleet as a safe haven during hurricanes. Each skipper has his own piling driven deep into the mud and around which his boat can pivot without hitting another vessel.

Joe Milliner, proprietor of the general store, told me that the high marsh by the road once served as the village baseball diamond. That was up to about 1925, when most every American town that could field nine able-bodied men had its own team. During the past seven decades, mean sea level has risen at least six inches, and the upper end of the marsh has subsided as well. At the same time, the lower marsh eroded into the estuary, delta-style, and I now own several acres more than did my predecessors a century ago. Today, it would be impossible to lay out a baseball diamond in the upper marsh without crossing at least one muskrat run and encompassing several sinkholes.

A small consequence of the rising sea and subsiding marsh is that muskrats build few houses today across the road. When we first came here, dozens of mounds of grass, sedge, and mud, five feet across and three feet high, dotted the meandering margins and small oxbow peninsulas of Rattrap Creek. The marsh was still high enough and the flow of Rattrap Creek still strong enough to support a variety of plants tolerant of low-salinity water. Big cordgrass, threesquare rush, cattail, pickerelweed, arrow arum, and smartweeds were all eaten and used in home construction by the black-furred muskrats. Increasingly, however, Rattrap Creek has been sucked up to irrigate adjoining farm fields and the sea frequently floods areas of the marsh that once rarely tasted saltwater. The rushes and sedges have given way to gall bush and saltwort, and the continual flooding combined with occasionally severe winter freezing killed many muskrats in their dens and drove survivors to tunnel in the dikes and other higher portions of the marsh.

Elsewhere, formerly dominant salt meadow hay now shares the landscape with extensive patches of black needlerush and even broader areas of salt marsh cordgrass. Such subtle ecological changes may have affected other wildlife species, including the tiny and secretive black rail. Ecologists blame the black rail's decline on man-made habitat degradation, but what if marsh subsidence was also at work? What if a gradually rising sea converted countless high-ground acres of salt meadow hay into lower, wetter, and more marginal black rail habitat?

William Burt in *Shadowbirds* (1994) reports that early egg collectors found most of their black rail nests in salt meadow hay. If subsidence in our marsh is typical of what has happened elsewhere along the Atlantic coast, countless acres of salt meadow hay have been replaced by needlerush and cordgrass. The marsh is still viable, but its altered ecology has had an adverse impact on the black rail. Fortunately, our marsh still has enough salt meadow hay to support some of these rare birds. Les Line, the former editor of *Audubon,* saw his first-ever black rail running across the causeway in front of our house. In 1992, a black rail was flushed in our marsh by George Armistead and two other triple-A birders during the local Christmas Bird Count.

So long as salt marshes flood and drain twice a day, so long as they remain unpolluted, there's no reason that people can't visit and even consume their renewable resources the way birds do. Each spring, I set traps for mummichogs (an Indian word that means "they go in great numbers" but which may also refer to silversides and other school bait fish).* They are also called killifish (a Dutch word referring to the estuarine streams, or "kills," where the little fishes are found) or, as the local watermen call and occasionally spell all members of the Cyprinodontidae, "bull minnas." In April and May, summer flounder return from spawning grounds at the edge of the continental shelf to feed in the warmer waters draining the marsh. Since flounder feed more by sight than scent, they're usually as ready to attack lures as they are bait. However, there are days when flounder are slow to seize a jig bouncing along the bottom; then, nothing works better than a lip-hooked, wriggling mummichog.

Two creeks flow into the marsh on either side of our property. The one nearest the house provides a steady supply of mummichogs most of the year, although spring offers the best trapping, with dozens of fat, egg-filled females adored by male mummichogs, flounder fishermen, bitterns, snowy and great egrets, green herons, night herons, and great and little blue herons alike. What we adore, however, is not always what's best for us. Mummichogs are loaded with the enzyme thiaminase, which destroys thiamine, otherwise known as vitamin B_1. Thiaminase may act as an antifreeze, enabling mummichogs to revive after being locked in winter mud, but most warm-blooded creatures cannot live long without vitamin

---

* Five Atlantic coastal fishes are still identified by their Indian names: mummichog, menhaden (poghaden or pogy), scuppaug or scup (porgy), squeteague (weakfish), and tautog. Curiously, these names are all derived from the Narragansett dialect of the Algonquian language.

B_1. That's why winter-bound herons forced to feed exclusively on mummichogs in ice-free holes in tidal streams often convulse and die after a number of days. The cold is not killing the birds; the mummichogs are.

Even when the spring flounder run is over, I frequently keep my funnel traps in Finney Creek to see what else the tides will bring. Although experts argue over the best bait to use for minnows—fish heads, crushed clams or crabs, squid or bacon suet—no bait is actually necessary as long as the trap is made of galvanized metal. Plastic minnow traps may last longer, but their lighter weight allows them to drift in a current. Bait fish are not as susceptible to plastic traps not only because of such drifting but also because plastic doesn't provide the metallic appeal of galvanized zinc gradually dissolving in brackish water. The irony is that just as too many mummichogs are poisonous to herons, too much zinc is poisonous to mummichogs. In fact, zinc is highly toxic to all aquatic organisms. But, as in other aspects of life, that may be part of its appeal.

Whether drawn by the chemistry of metallic decay or mere curiosity, once one mummichog is in the trap, others follow, possibly attracted by the pheromones of the first fish. My unbaited traps soon fill, not just with mummichogs, but with an assortment of juvenile Sciaenidae—including spot, croaker, and drum—fiddler and baby blue crabs, small eels, and an occasional water snake that slithers in at low tide to feast on the barely submerged bait fish but then, trapped, drowns as the tide returns.

My favorite fish caught in the traps—but always released because they don't survive long as bait—are sheepshead minnows. Stubby and pugnacious, with breeding hues of metallic green, blue, and salmon, the male sheepshead minnow makes an interesting aquarium specimen. This species, along with the mosquito fish, black-banded sunfish, and pygmy sunfish, was the subject of my first freelance article written for *The Aquarium* while I was still an undergraduate at Princeton. Part of the sheepshead minnow's appeal lies in its close relationship to five species of endangered pupfishes whose desert-waterhole habitats in California, Nevada, and Texas were once part of a vast inland sea. Pupfishes are relict reminders of an ancient ocean, just as the sheepshead minnow is a harbinger of a not geologically distant future when the Atlantic will once again inundate the coastal plain.

My favorite mammal in the marsh is the otter. Thanks to the convergence here of two watersheds, two pairs of otters sometimes frequent the upper marsh. A less productive habitat would be fortunate to have a single pair merely wander through. Since both parents care for their one to four offspring for up to a year, I see more otter sign, and sometimes the animals themselves, when I walk the dikes separating our freshwater ponds from the marsh than I see raccoons, although raccoons greatly outnumber otters.

I know that because I trap raccoons to reduce their predatory pressure on locally nesting birds, especially ducks and clapper rail; because raccoons raid and rip apart my birdseed and suet feeders in winter and dig into and scatter my compost piles year-round; and because two raccoons can do more wanton damage to a field of corn than

a herd of deer. Naturalist E. Lawrence Palmer once estimated that "suitable woodland of 200 acres can support a
raccoon population which will give a sustained yield of 1
raccoon a year." Yet a dozen acres alone along Finney
Creek support enough animals to provide an annual yield
of half a dozen raccoons. Indeed, the density of these animals is so great on the Eastern Shore that Virginia Tech
researcher George Simmons found several seemingly pris-
tine watersheds severely contaminated with *E. coli*—a bac-
terium usually associated with untreated human sewage,
but here a by-product of raccoon feces.

The harder I work to control them, the more I seem to
attract. They prey on everything from spawning salaman-
ders to winter-stressed woodcock. I'm reminded of naturalist John Burroughs' remark that whenever he shot a
groundhog, six came to its funeral. I trap raccoons for the
same reason Burroughs shot groundhogs. He was protecting a garden that sustained him both aesthetically and
nutritionally. I tend a larger "garden" for the same reasons.
If I stopped trapping and let nature take its course, the
farm would soon lose much of its diversity.

I don't trap otters, although in many ways they're superior predators to raccoons. A pair once killed a nesting
Canada goose near the house. On another occasion, I saw
a big male torpedo through the shallows toward an unsus-
pecting hooded merganser, which escaped at the last
moment by leaping straight into the air like a teal. Some
ornithologists might say that mergansers are physically
incapable of leaping straight into the air; they must run
along the water to take off. But that hooded merganser

wasn't the first creature (or person) I've seen do the impossible when its life was at stake.

Otters make a mockery of fishery management. All formulas concerning the proper balance of bass and bluegill, or the advice to avoid introducing crappie unless you have ample forage fishes to support them, are overthrown by the tag-team assaults of otters underwater and herons, kingfishers, and ospreys from above. Birds represent only seasonal pressure, but the otters eat bass, bluegill, crappie, white perch, and whatever else I stock or stocks itself as soon as such fish reach sufficient size to attract the otters' interest.

If we could only work together, I wouldn't mind so much. I once found a four-pound largemouth bass pulled up on the bank with her gills and guts—probably roe sacks—eaten. The flesh was untouched but too putrid to salvage. If the otter had delivered this already cleaned but in-fresher-condition fish to my back door, I'd feel less frustration in watching families of otters make search-and-destroy sweeps of my ponds.

If I were to take up otter trapping, I have in my library an excellent how-to book on the subject written by a local pastor. When the Reverend W. J. "Jack" Milliner, Jr., was a young man, he supplemented his farm income by trapping otters in the marshes around Locustville. In 1961, he published a now rare volume called *Fooling Mr. Otter*. Part of the book's interest lies in its photographs, many of which were taken by another local celebrity, David Corson, whose photograph of a basset hound helped raise Hush Puppies from relative obscurity to one of the best-known shoe companies in the nation.

Jack Milliner no longer traps otters, and a clue as to why lies in his book's title. Otters have personality. The larger males—five feet long, weighing thirty pounds, and a third again larger than their lifetime mates—command the respect inherent in the word *Mister*. Otters may wear the gold standard of aquatic fur—pelts that are both beautiful and durable—but they elicit a fondness and admiration we don't usually feel for other members of the weasel clan. My greatest respect stems from the fact that, unlike most other mammals, otters usually live longer in the wild than they do in captivity.

After nearly a quarter century at the upper end of this estuary, I've seen more change in the marsh than continuity. Some of these changes I've been able to monitor with duck blinds. Every half dozen years or so, I build a new blind for guests. I use exterior-grade plywood for the walls and anchor the structure with half a dozen pressure-treated posts driven well into the mud. It makes little difference. No tidal blind lasts for long. If storms don't destroy it, the marsh simply moves away. One island on which a blind was located drifted more than thirty yards downstream.

Rather than fear nature's capricious power, I'm enthralled by it. My life, my ambition, are nothing to the rising sea. Tides will one day cross the causeway, and otters will chase fish among the tombstones in our cemetery. Herons will perch on what's left of the house's foundations and spear mummichogs where the boxwoods now grow. Thus, even while the wind whispers *de contemptu mundi*, each rising sun urges *carpe diem*.

CHAPTER 6

The Case of the Road-Killed Flounder

F or the first few years, we could visit the farm only on weekends, first from New York, later from Washington. When we arrived late on Friday evenings in the fall without having brought any food, my pride was in getting up early the next morning and returning with squirrels or a rabbit for breakfast and quail or a duck for

49

supper. Thanksgiving dinner was intentional potluck: Sometimes we ate as lean as a clapper rail; other times, as fat as a Canada goose.

One weekend I shot a Japanese green pheasant, a survivor or descendant of a state stocking effort that ended in the mid-1960s. Despite several public and many private attempts to establish pheasants below the Mason-Dixon line, and despite the fact that a few hang on by roosting in needlerush, where foxes are reluctant to forage, pheasants have too many predators here to reach the critical mass necessary to enable them to withstand attrition yet prevail the way bobwhite quail do.

Under the pressures of clean farming—which eliminates random hedgerows and overgrown ditches—and suburbanization—which provides increasing support for that supreme predator of ground-nesting birds, the house cat—even bobwhite quail are declining. Yet more and more local landowners are purposely providing habitat for quail. A few are doing what they can to control the cats, and if more farmers could be persuaded to go easy on the pesticides, the bobwhite might have a fighting chance. What worries me is that despite doing all these things myself, I still find fewer birds each fall on the farm than I did twenty years ago when I did little to support them. In the early 1970s, I often flushed five different coveys during an afternoon's walk; now I'm fortunate to find three.

Another puzzlement is the clapper rail. Throughout the 1970s, while rabbit and duck populations fluctuated, I could always count on rail for a subsistence supper. Marsh hens were abundant across the road, and if Barbara and I required more than our usual brace for dinner—usually because guests had come and wanted wild game—I'd canoe around the fringes of the estuary on a rising tide and shoot half a dozen more.* In those days, before we knew how contaminated with industrial residues the organs of most waterfowl had become, we diced, fried, and mixed with rice the hearts, livers, and gizzards of all the game birds we shot. We called this side dish "Dirty Rice," without any intimation of irony.

Gradually, almost imperceptibly, clapper rail declined. In 1977, the International Association of Fish and Wildlife Agencies published a book entitled *Management of Migratory Shore and Upland Game Birds in North America.* Its section on the Rallidae presented this Catch-22: Only increased hunting pressure would justify the research necessary to find out why most species of rail, coot, and gallinule were declining.

Although biologists believe that habitat destruction and industrial contamination are the main causes of these birds' decline, on the Eastern Shore of Virginia, where neither of these problems is significant, some of the clapper rail's woes may be linked to the advent of nesting colonies of herring gulls and great black-backed gulls. The swelling gull colonies are cheaper to control than habitat destruction, yet neither the U.S. Fish and Wildlife Service nor the commonwealth's Department of Game and Inland Fisheries is willing to challenge wildlife sentimen-

---

* The limit was, and is, "a total of 15 clapper rails and king rails, counted together a day, 30 in possession, and 25 sora and Virginia rails, counted together a day, 25 in possession."

talists who believe that every gull is named Jonathan Livingston.

Before we bought our farm in 1970, great black-backed gulls never bred on the Delmarva Peninsula, and herring gulls had only begun breeding near Chincoteague in the late 1960s. Both species had formerly visited Virginia only in the winter after leaving their traditional breeding grounds in maritime Canada and New England. Once established as breeders in Virginia, however, nesting colonies of both gulls have spread like cancer. The size of the great black-backed gull alone makes it a formidable predator. Gulls venture well out in the marsh to find clapper rail nests that foraging raccoons miss. And whereas raccoons go mostly for the eggs, black-backed gulls kill and eat the adult birds as well.

One spring I helped John Buckalew, the first manager of the Chincoteague National Wildlife Refuge, band nestling black-backed gulls that were already twice the size of adult laughing gulls. It was hot, buggy, and even hazardous work as the young gulls stabbed us with their beaks and smacked us with their wings. Why, I asked John, wouldn't it be more sensible to wring the little devils' necks while we had them in hand, and give much-needed relief to every other breeding bird in Virginia's coastal marshes, than to merely monitor their spread by banding them?

John was stunned by the question. Data are the building blocks of science. Yet mindlessly collecting data has become a substitute for what most biologists are no longer allowed to do: genuine wildlife management. The phrase "scientific management" is now an oxymoron. Biologists cannot be both "scientists" and "managers" if they cannot use the data they've compiled on the spread of a species such as the great black-backed gull to counter its adverse impact on other species that, historically, never had to endure black-backed gulls.

The decline of clapper rail through the 1980s was less apparent to southern coastal sportsmen than it should have been, because most had already turned to mourning doves for their late-summer recreation. Dove hunting is now *the* outdoor southern social event of September. When I was an undergraduate at Princeton, I told visiting writer William Faulkner that New Jersey categorized the mourning dove as a songbird, so we couldn't hunt it. He asked in genuine perplexity, "What do you do in September?"

Like most landowners who hunt, I grow a few acres of sunflowers each summer, as well as strips of proso, brown-top, and Japanese millet, specifically to attract dove. Such plantings also attract goldfinches, cardinals, and a variety of sparrows, as well as the kestrels and sharp-shinned hawks that feed on them. Dove are generally too quick to be caught by hawks, although I did once see a Cooper's hawk take a mourning dove on the ground.

I may shoot fifty dove a season; guests sometimes shoot two hundred more.[*] That sounds like a lot until you learn that more mourning dove are shot each year in the United States than all other migratory game birds combined. One recent estimate was 49.4 million. Starting with an average

---

[*] The limit is twelve per day, twenty-four in possession.

of forty nesting pairs on or near the farm, my local dove population may climb to three hundred by the end of the summer. Whether or not I shoot any that fall, they're back to forty nesting pairs the following spring. The average annual turnover across the nation, regardless of whether hunting is allowed, is between 65 and 80 percent. Since the mourning dove seems to be the feathered equivalent of Al Capp's Schmoo, why not let hunters in every state tap it for food and recreation?

Some days, when nonhunting guests are expected for dinner and the dove are feeding elsewhere, I shoot and pluck a couple of dozen red-winged blackbirds, grackles, or starlings, which also come to the sunflower fields. If guests are open-minded, I tell them what they're eating. If not, they end up praising Barbara's "sora rail casserole."

Our farm is bisected by two county roads: that means annual litter by the ton and roadkill by the dozens. Although we've long been able to collect and sell the aluminum beverage cans tossed in the ditches, only recently have we been able to recycle the glass and plastic trash as well. Altogether, my son and I use my pickup to carry away more than four truckloads a year. Not bad for only three-quarters of a mile of road. Our compensation comes in two forms: An average annual aluminum recycling income of $40 and an occasional bonus of four or five still-intact cans or bottles of beer from a six-pack discarded by an underage drinker who probably figured he'd be less conspicuous buying a six-pack but panicked at the

thought that his parents might find the extra cans or bottles in the car.*

Animals killed on the road are soon recycled by other
animals. Sadly, screech owls are common car victims. They
often hunt mice on the shoulders, where too many night
drivers stray. I've probably contributed to this motorized
mayhem by erecting nesting boxes in the swamp adjoining
the road and planting hedges and filter strips along both
corridors. More wildlife now lives next to our roads than
when they were bracketed by open fields, so more wildlife
also dies there.

Attrition is evenhanded: Predators die in proportion to
prey. Although I mostly find crushed rabbits, mangled
muskrats, and flattened songbirds, I also occasionally discover battered opossums, smashed raccoons, and squished
black rat snakes. Once a year, a red or gray fox is killed in
front of the house, and I once found the broken-backed
body of an otter on the causeway around the bend. Yet the
saddest victims for me are the pond and box turtles. Their
shells, which work so well to protect them from natural
predators, explode when struck by the tires of a careless
motorist.

In the late 1960s, the Humane Society of the United
States tried to sensitize Americans to the terrible toll we

---

* The mid-January 1994 issue of *Farm Journal* quoted me as follows: "I find
more beer cans and liquor bottles than soft-drink cans on my property. There
aren't that many more beer drinkers; it's just that people are more willing to
save their cola cans and recycle them. The guy who polishes off five beers at
lunch doesn't want to be reminded that he has a problem."

inflict on wildlife with our vehicles. Volunteers in various parts of the country surveyed sections of road during a holiday weekend, and the society estimated that at least a million "animals"—meaning major species such as antelope and armadillos, not minor ones such as birds and butterflies—died across the nation every twenty-four hours. Press releases were sent to all the media, but editors and news anchors decided that since there was nothing we could do about the problem—short of reducing our reliance on cars—it was too sad a story to tell.

Unable to prevent the slaughter of wildlife on even the short sections of road that run through my farm, I do the next best thing: I salvage what I can. In the 1970s, I had a federal permit that allowed me to pick up dead songbirds that were later used in adult education classes at the Smithsonian Institution. Eventually, however, I got tired of filling out the papers that sometimes weighed more than the songbirds themselves.

Today, I use only my state hunting license to salvage whatever game I find in season. In Virginia, even this isn't required to salvage a road-killed deer. A car-bashed deer becomes the property of anyone who notifies a state trooper or warden to come tag it. Although it's customary to offer the carcass to the driver, he may not be in any condition to accept it. On the other side of town, I once watched two truck drivers fight over the hindquarters of a car-mutilated buck. When the struggle was over, one of the men had to be loaded into an ambulance along with the guy who had hit the deer in the first place.

There's an ethic to living off the road just as there is to living off the land. Unwritten rules dictate that you must avoid hitting anything yourself, but you should stop to dispatch any severely injured animal you see. Even as I write this, however, I realize what a hopeless suggestion this is for most people. Denial is our species' most common characteristic. If we didn't have the capacity to deny something unpleasant or shameful—to erase it completely from our memory banks—we'd have to live with the guilt of what we'd done. I can't imagine anyone with more than a few years' driving experience who hasn't killed wildlife, yet rarely do I hear anyone admit that he or she has done so.

I was riding with an avid birder one day when he struck a female indigo bunting. He stopped the car, but when we heard the male bunting singing off the side of the road, he decided that he must have missed the bird even though I was positive he'd hit it. When we got back to his house, I found the bunting stuck in the car radiator. I decided to save it for a Smithsonian class, and I thought that my companion would be keen to see an indigo bunting close up. Instead, the guy became bug-eyed with denial! He not only didn't want to see the bird, he wouldn't let me bring it into his house. To this day, he insists that I'm lying if I try to remind him of the incident.

One night I horrified an acquaintance when I pulled off the road to go back with a flashlight to find a feral cat I'd just hit. When I found the writhing animal, I used a tire iron to dispatch it. It was a gruesome task made no easier by my companion's ravings about how he hoped I'd go straight to hell for such savagery. I was thinking just the opposite: That anyone who shirked his responsibility to a suffering animal was the real candidate for eternal damnation.

The most unusual roadkill I can recall occurred one weekend when Barbara was counting on me to supply dinner. After a fruitless trek through the woods up Finney Creek and an empty swing across the fields to Rattrap Creek, I decided to make things easier on my dog and myself by walking home along the road from Onley. As we approached its intersection with the road into Locustville, a seafood truck came speeding around the corner and spilled a basket off the tailgate. The basket broke open and scattered blue crabs and fish for thirty yards along the pavement. I saw a big flounder flopping in the middle of the road and began jogging toward it just as a car following the truck ran over it. When I reached the fish, I was relieved to see that the auto had crushed the flounder's head but left its fillets undamaged. Slipping the fish into my game bag, I proceeded to fill the rest of my vest with crabs. With this satisfying weight tugging at my shoulders, Rocky and I finished our stroll home.

Just as we turned into the driveway, Joe Milliner drove by. As an avid bird hunter, Joe wanted to know how I'd done.

"No quail," I said, "but I got a nice flounder and a dozen crabs."

Joe looked incredulous until I showed him my booty, whereupon he looked even more incredulous. I told him what had happened and suggested that if he hurried along, there might still be some crabs left.

"I'm not picking any crabs off the road!" he said.

"It's easier than picking them out of a crab pot."

"No, thank you! I'll buy my seafood at the market."

I should probably be grateful that most people feel the way Joe does. If everyone started salvaging roadkills, there might not be enough to go around.

CHAPTER 7

The Restorer

"No home can survive without people living there," says Bill Belote. "Even squatters who chip chair rails and carve their initials in the banisters are better than boarding the place up and letting the weather and vines work their way in."

Bill cares deeply about old homes. There's hardly a historic structure in either county of Virginia's Eastern Shore that he hasn't worked on. That's why it's odd that he appears to live nowhere in particular himself. His home of the moment is always the building he's restoring. Even Bill's son, Ted, and his half-brother, Shirley—who may or may not share the workday with him—rarely know where he or they will be from one morning to the next.

"If it's raining when you get up," Bill may tell them, "I'll be up to the Mapp Place. If it clears, I'll be down to Vaucluse."

"The trouble is," Shirley complains, "it may be clear in his corner of the county, but raining over by me or Ted."

"What happens then?" I ask.

"We go to work where we think he'll be. He's there or he's not. If he needs us, he'll come fetch us. But he does a fair bit of work by himself."

Such a random approach to restoration would cripple the reputation and prospects of a less talented team than the Belotes. But their magic is so well known from Cape Charles to above the Maryland line that if they were willing to work more than an hour's drive from Ted's or Shirley's home in central Accomack, they could easily quadruple both their work and their hourly rates.

This was especially true after I profiled Bill in the January/February 1988 issue of *Historic Preservation*. Readers called him from as far away as Kentucky, promising him every conceivable perk if he'd come and restore their homes. A wealthy widow in Washington, D.C., hinted at even greater favors if he'd redo her floors. Fortunately for us on the Eastern Shore, Bill has never had a desire to be anywhere else, especially after he saw some of those somewhere elses as a navy boatswain mate during World War II.

Bill selects his projects, first, on the basis of how interesting the work will be; next, on whether he likes the owners; and last and truly least, on how much money he'll make. We could afford to pay him only $3 an hour when we started, and $2 each for Ted and Shirley. We also paid $1 an hour to an occasional hod carrier who might have done better on welfare but whose pride forbade it.

Pride is the principal thread of the southern cultural tapestry—a pride that includes making do with what you have. From an early age, I saw that pride as something that distinguished my mother from many of the New Yorkers among whom she'd come to live. I also saw it in the Belotes—in Bill's scorn for building inspectors and tax assessors who weigh only the quantity, never the quality, of what they inspect or assess; and in Shirley's scoffing at a federal agency that insisted local farmers supply migrant laborers with flush toilets when some farmers themselves still lacked that amenity. Shirley installed his own first flush toilet with money he earned on the job with us. At the Grand Opening, as Shirley called it, each guest was asked to help initiate the new facility.

Southern pride is rooted in the region's collective memory, real and romantic, of the Civil War and the alleged Golden Age that preceded it. Virginia's Eastern Shore was occupied early by the Union Army, which is the reason that so many antebellum homes survived. Also surviving is the area's independent-mindedness and the local people's willingness to make or grow whatever they need or to go without. Bill is like his ancestors—the first Belote arrived in 1647—in forging the hinges or lamps he needs for a restoration rather than buying factory-produced replicas. When he was younger, he also cut and milled local loblolly pine to duplicate a fractured piece of heartwood rather than buy soft, plantation-grown yellow pine that, even with staining, never quite matches.

Bill worked for the better part of five years on our farm while Barbara and I were disengaging ourselves from Manhattan and then the District of Columbia. Bill liked seeing us only on weekends; it left him free to restore the house as his own. Sometimes this saved us money, as when he removed an old joist from the floor below the kitchen and spliced it into a damaged beam above. Other times, such authenticity was expensive, as when Ted made a light-switch plate from a piece of antique siding so that its grain would match the library paneling perfectly. It was something that only we would notice, but Barbara and I shared the Belotes' pride in their craftsmanship.

Controversy swirls around the origins of the lower Shore's architecture. Academic authority H. Chandlee Forman suggests that the area's most characteristic homes—those built only one room deep with steeply pointed gables, batten or board doors, "walk-in" fireplaces, and winding, "break-your-neck" staircases—echo the Middle Ages. And some features of certain old homes, such as the outside row of "sqynchon" (chamfered or beveled) bricks at Evergreen—the first house Bill Belote ever worked on—are reminiscent of medieval England.

But local historian L. Floyd Nock III contends that it's simpler than that: "There were only three variables that determined pre-Industrial Revolution architecture: Climate, availability of materials, and the local economy. Early Eastern Shore homes were built only one room deep because the English who settled here were from a colder, damper climate. They did all they could architecturally to utilize Virginia's warmer temperatures and salubrious breezes.

"Our houses are mostly wood, because the Shore was covered by a great forest. The superior grades found in all the early buildings are proof that the colonists burned for fuel, or left to rot, anything that wasn't of architectural quality. Stone in any size is rare on the Shore, so only one early stone house is known, and that was made with imported material. Our local clays are of such poor quality, our bricks came mostly from Maryland or the Western Shore. The most important factor distinguishing early Eastern Shore homes from domestic architecture elsewhere in the southern colonies is that by the beginning of the eighteenth century, the Shore had developed a sizable middle class—farmers, fishermen, traders of livestock and grain—most of them living in modest homes."

The economies of Accomack and Northampton Counties still reflect the family farming and fishing traditions that ensured the colonists' survival and eventually provided them with their first affluence. Belote is a Dutch or Flemish name, and throughout the seventeenth century, the Eastern Shore conducted an extensive intercolonial and overseas trade with Holland quite independent of the rest of Virginia. County records—which in Northampton extend back to 1632—show that local trade with New Amsterdam continued even after the British Crown forbade it.

Despite or because of its self-sufficiency, the Eastern Shore has long been regarded by the rest of Virginia as a cultural backwater. Indeed, some Virginians and most Americans don't even know there is a Virginia Eastern Shore. I recently visited the University of Virginia, where permanent wall maps with pegs for notes are used by students looking for rides home. The map for the commonwealth has no Eastern Shore. Presumably anyone wishing to come here hangs his or her note on the eastern half of the map of Maryland.

Such unfamiliarity can be a blessing for those who value antiquities, because what's not known about is not pulled down to make way for tract homes and shopping centers. Shaped by the ocean with many little bays, rivers, creeks, and tidal guts, much of the lower Shore seems designed for small farms and villages paradoxically separated by land but joined by water.

In the early days, regular contact was maintained by sail, lighter, and the log canoes that Indians taught the colonists to build. Until the 1650s, only a few hundred whites lived on the lower Shore. Their modest numbers didn't threaten the more numerous Indians. The Eastern Shore, therefore, missed most of the bloodshed and horror associated with Opechancanough's mainland uprising in 1644. By 1646, the Powhatan Confederacy was broken, and the demoralized tribes stoically accepted the growing presence of white settlers throughout Tidewater Virginia.

But about that time, the persecution of the Eastern Shore tribes began in earnest. In 1659, Edmund Scarburgh and Philip Taylor recruited whites from the Western Shore to cross the bay and help them hunt down the last Assateagues in the northern end of Accomack. This suggests that local whites had no stomach for the wanton slaughter. Bill Belote views these pogroms as a personal loss and shame.

"Our ancestors shared an earthly paradise with the Indians," he observes, "and not realizing it, they allowed it to be destroyed by the evil deeds of a few rapacious men, just because they were white."

Bill's affinity with the ecologically compatible but now extinct tribes is seen in his own humble lifestyle and the fact that he has one of the largest collections of Native American artifacts in eastern Virginia. Like most dedicated amateurs, Bill's records of precisely where and when he found each of his carefully numbered projectile points, scrapers, shaft smoothers, grindstones, and pottery shards are more detailed than comparable records kept by museums. The only trouble is that he's misplaced his code book. Bill believes that it's in a dresser drawer or cabinet at one of the places he worked on, or where friends have allowed him to store old furniture. He's confident that, sooner or later, the book will turn up. Meanwhile, he goes on marking newly found artifacts from a memory that puts a computer to shame.

Bill often uses lunch breaks to wander the edges of a property, picking up points, pipe stems, and pottery shards by the pocketful. When he was working on our farm, I used to join him in a nearby field above a stream where we found parts of a large and curiously patterned clay bowl. Over the years, as the farmer continued working the land, more shards worked their way to the surface, and Bill found enough of the bowl to reconstruct more than a third of it and even to fashion a replica.

Bill's eye for spotting artifacts is extraordinary. Once when I was chauffeuring him across a cornfield at about twenty miles an hour, he asked me to stop and back up because he'd just seen an arrowhead between the rows. Although I scrutinized the place he indicated, I couldn't see the finely sculptured quartzite piece until Bill got out to pick it up.

The annihilation of the Indians was an obsession for men like Edmund Scarburgh, because he couldn't cajole or threaten them into working for him. The Crown had acknowledged the Indians' right to land, and that right would disappear only when the Indians did. Unlike the Massachusetts Bay colonists, who were mostly educated men who had made a commitment to the New World by bringing their families with them, a few too many early Virginians were freebooters hoping to carve out fortunes and return to England, where they could buy the political rank and prestige previously denied them. Although the majority of Eastern Shore colonists were yeomen farmers who, like their New England counterparts, wanted only to live in harmony with the Indians and at peace with God, history documents the excesses of each generation's worst children.

The live-and-let-live attitude of Virginia's colonial majority enabled the unconscionable few to assemble vast property holdings. Edmund Scarburgh began in 1633 with two patents of 200 acres each. By 1660, he lay claim to over 30,000 acres. Such vast holdings, however, would have been more burden than blessing in the seventeenth century, since even a large family could work only a small plot of cleared land—unless they owned slaves.

So long as the Dutch controlled New York and New Jersey, Scarburgh could trade tobacco for African labor so that he could clear more land to grow more tobacco and acquire more Africans. Once the Dutch were expelled from the New World, however, Scarburgh had to compete with his better-connected rivals living along the James, York, and Rappahannock Rivers. From the 1660s on, Eastern Shore landowners began reducing their holdings. By the end of the seventeenth century, the average-size Accomack County plantation was 520 acres; in Northampton County, it was only 389 acres.

Such early history is important, not only because it reveals much about how politics and economics worked (and still work) in Tidewater Virginia but also because it explains what happened on the Eastern Shore once the demographic hub of the colony shifted to the west. Increasingly isolated, Eastern Shoremen changed less in their lives—including their architecture—than Western Shoremen. Today, the Eastern Shore is still made up of mostly small to middle-sized farms hewed from once large landholdings and, in some cases, still worked by descendants of the original settlers.

Surprisingly few names dominate the local phone book. There are 36 Justices, for example, but also 45 Justises. Is there any doubt they're descended from the same man? Similar sound-alikes include Kelley (32) and Kelly (29); Killmon (55) and Kilmon (19); and, of course, Scarburgh (1), Scarbrough (1), Scarbough (1), and Scarborough (27). I wouldn't be surprised if DNA tests revealed that even the Killmons, Kilmons, and Kellams (132) share a common ancestor, or that the Taylors (279) and the Tylers (14) do.

After the American Revolution, when a seller's market for the new nation's raw materials opened abroad, a building boom occurred on the lower Shore. Many so-called colonial homes were actually built during this postcolonial period, but because the homes have more early Georgian and even Jacobean features than Federalist ones, they appear older than they are.

Some seventeenth-century structures were torn down during this first American building boom to utilize their materials in new structures on the same sites. Bill Belote remembers that when he began work on Evergreen in about 1950, there were still quite a few homes whose odd mixtures of architecture spanned three centuries. At Evergreen, for example, Bill found where a 1680s brick wall had been sheared off to blend into a 1780s room. It was such a striking feature that Bill decided to expose the old wall during the restoration. He looked through old county records and learned that a Dr. George Hack had lived on the site before 1665. When Adam Muir tore down the structure in the 1780s and built his own house, his builder was thrifty enough to incorporate the brick corner from the Hack House into the new wall of the Muir House.

Bill often wonders about those early, mostly anonymous builders. He has come to recognize a number of their unique styles in the different places he's worked. Even when a builder failed to leave an identifying design or "signature" in an eave terminal, Bill may recognize other ingredients that link the origins of one house to those of another. The eave terminals in our farmhouse, for example, resemble a cookie-cutter profile of Daffy Duck's head. There's no other way to describe the curious design. Two other buildings in the immediate area had similar eave terminals, but when they were razed for their lumber, Barbara and I assumed that our home was the only surviving specimen of this particular builder's handiwork.

One morning Bill told us in his soft-spoken way that he'd been poking around an old house well up the Seaside Road. He was fairly certain that the man who'd built that house had also built ours. I asked him if the eave terminals were identical.

"No," he replied.

"Then how can you be sure?"

"Nothing I can put my finger on," he said. "There's just something about the proportions of the house, the way the wood's been cut and pegged, the pattern of the mullions and sashes, that makes me certain the same man built both."

Bill's ability to identify with the ghosts of builders past has provided some wonderful rebates for the owners of the homes he's restored. When he was at Evergreen, he was dissatisfied with an existing chair rail, convinced that the original had been something quite different. He didn't tamper with the rail for many weeks while he worked around it and finished other rooms in the house. Then one day he found a piece of an ancient rail bracing a sagging joist in the attic. Bill felt sure that it was the missing pattern and confirmed it by matching nail holes in the wall. Since the old rail was unique, Bill used his antique carpentry tools to duplicate the rail from salvaged lengths of comparably old wood. It was a lot of trouble, to be sure, but Bill finished the room and the house knowing that he'd restored a special ingredient of the original builder's design.

Bill is known, even notorious, for resisting the tendency of an owner to "upscale" an old but modest home into something more grand and pretentious. Bill will pretend to be hard of hearing while an owner—possibly inspired by a recent visit to Williamsburg—goes on about arched doorways and elaborately carved mantels. Bill patiently insists that every modification should be "in keeping" with the intention and budget of the original builder. If the new owner doesn't take the hint, Bill simply stops work and moves elsewhere.

Bill's not always adamant. He accepted my suggestion, for instance, that we turn one room of our obviously non-literary farmhouse into a library. When the wallpaper was stripped away, Bill found his idea for the shelves and lower storage cabinets in the vertical paneling discovered under the crinkled layers around the fireplace. By Williamsburg standards, the paneling is crude and seemingly improvised, as though the owner had run out of money after shooting the moon on triple-thick brick foundations and a paved cellar. The builder used ordinary beaded weatherboarding for the paneling and framed the fireplace with an unadorned mantel. So, likewise, Bill made his new cabinets from old beaded weatherboard and even attached the cabinet door hinges on the outside, just as his predecessor had done 160 years earlier.

Despite the fact that old homes represent the most desirable real estate, notable structures continue to disappear at an alarming rate. Floyd Nock has a photographic record of dozens of fine structures in Accomack and Northampton Counties that were lost even as he was assembling his archive.

"Seaview, Marino, and Goshen were burned by arsonists," Floyd recalls, "but their loss is no more painful than Shabby Hall, Gargaphia Savannah, and Bellevue—the first two moved to a so-called restoration village in Maryland, and the other torn down for its paneling."

Shabby Hall was a particular loss for Locustville, since it anchored the upper end of our village just as our home anchors the lower. It was built in the late 1700s by an ambitious young man who went to Baltimore to find a wife. She was allegedly so disappointed when she saw what he'd advertised as his "plantation" that she named it "Shabby Hall." Nevertheless, they lived there happily ever after.

Two years after we bought our home, about the time that other young couples began appearing on the Shore to find old places to fix up, a man with a different dream appeared. Perry Van Vleck decided that rather than make people come to the Shore to restore old homes, he'd take the old homes to them. He created a development not far from Washington, D.C., known as Lower Marlboro Towne. He took various sections of old Eastern Shore houses that he had sawn apart and loaded them onto trucks and barges and ferried them across the Chesapeake to his development. Once there, the pieces were crowded onto lots and tacked together with plywood and pegboard like architectural versions of Frankenstein's monster. Van Vleck paid up to $1,500 for each building and another $25,000 to move it; he sold the reassembled structures for between $250,000 and $300,000 each. He called his project a labor of love, but like many labors and loves, his efforts were misplaced, for once an old structure is taken from the land, the site loses its historic context and becomes just another property that is as suitable for a trailer park as for preservation.

Land is the key to southern culture. You cannot comprehend an old home anywhere from Maryland to Texas without first contemplating the land from which it grew. Yet increasing numbers of old southern homes no longer draw nourishment from their surroundings. Even when they're not hemmed in by housing projects, historic homes are maintained as museums and sit surreally in little parks, where lawns substitute for the crops that once gave the homes their income and meaning. In the old days, when a new roof was needed, some product of the land was sold. Nowadays, taxpayers foot the bill. Such preservation is ritual without meaning; it's like perpetuating endangered species in a zoo.

Although Bill Belote does much of his work for homeowners like us, he finds time for the less lucrative but more prestigious work of public restoration. In recent years, the Belote team has put a new roof on the chamber of commerce building (originally an early-nineteenth-century mercantile and customs office), pointed up the brick at the debtors' prison (an eighteenth-century jailor's residence converted to a prison for debtors in 1824), and restuccoed the Episcopal church in Accomac (a structure dating to 1838). In addition, the Belotes restored Brownsville, an 1806 residence that's now the headquarters for the Virginia Coast Reserve of the Nature Conservancy.

Although Bill believes it is important to maintain such public and semipublic buildings, he often finds himself in conflict with the committees in charge. "An appointed group," he says, "is never as willing to put sufficient money into restoration as a private citizen into something he owns. Unless we can persuade people to buy and live in old buildings, we'll lose them. And the best way to persuade people to live in historic homes is to provide tax incentives for them to do so."

Old county records tell us who paid what taxes on certain structures, but they rarely tell us anything about the builders who created them. Even today, garden-tour brochures announce that the so-and-sos restored such-and-such, when actually the so-and-sos only provided the funds for unremembered artisans to do the work. In the half century since Bill Belote returned from military service in the Pacific, he has worked on dozens of historic structures and been given credit for few of them. Like a medieval builder raising cathedrals to the glory of God and a more humble habitation for himself, Bill accepts anonymity as the master builder's fate. Like those anonymous builders of yore, Bill realizes that spiritual salvation begins with meaningful work, and that the pursuit of money and fame only distracts us from the greater goal of personal fulfillment. He believes that his spirit, if not the memory of him as an individual, will survive so long as dozens of distinguished Eastern Shore structures survive. That is his consolation and his only vanity.

CHAPTER 8

Artifacts

Restoring an old home can be melancholy work. As you peel away the past, you find that each layer of wallpaper symbolizes a generation of hope whose outcome you know but are helpless to alter. Barbara and I paid our respects by taking pictures, making notes, and saving a brittle swatch or two.

Each layer in what's now the library evoked a different era. The pattern put up after World War II was a triumphal blend of purple, pink and aquamarine. It was also "Guaranteed Washable, Fadeproof, Wall-Tested, Style-Tested, Made in U.S.A." Before World War I, fewer promises were made, but more may have been kept; the era is summed up in a modest display of peach stripes and green dots. Below that, late-nineteenth-century conservatism is captured in a beige mesh design. And earliest of all, a simple pattern of pale roses stirs memories of a quiet confidence in the rural South before the Civil War.

Northern visitors generally show less appreciation for the house's antiquity than our southern guests. My editor at Prentice-Hall initiated the sport of smashing blood-gorged mosquitoes against the kitchen wall, signing his name, dating the deed, and then drawing a cameolike circle around the spot. By the end of the second summer, the kitchen had become a parody of Sardi's, with some of the most celebrated names in New York film and publishing scribbled under the remains of squashed mosquitoes. Barbara and I should have saved those signatures, either with a camera or by removing particularly choice sections of wallpaper. But one winter weekend, we came down from the city and found that the Belotes had shifted their operations into the kitchen, taken down the spotted walls, and used the broken plaster to fill holes in the clamshell driveway. *Sic transit gloria.*

Although the previous owner sold all the old decoys once stashed in the henhouse, I discovered beneath its floorboards the rotted body of a hooded merganser hen carved by Ira Hudson. He was born in Delaware in 1876 and moved to Chincoteague just before the turn of the century. During his lifetime, Hudson was better known as a boatbuilder than a decoy carver, but since few of his boats survive and far fewer people collect boats than decoys, he and the Cobb family of Northampton County are remembered today as Virginia's most notable links to the heyday of decoy carving and market hunting.

Although the federal government stopped all commercial shooting in 1918, local pockets of resistance have continued to the present. In 1987, an Accomack man was prosecuted for shooting and selling several thousand divers (mostly redheads) and blackducks. The irony of America's prohibitionist approach to waterfowl management—we now have the most restrictive regulations of any nation on earth—is that American wildfowlers have seen their daily bag limit dwindle from twenty-five ducks in the early 1920s to three today, and their season is down from four months to one. Despite such restrictions, North American duck populations, especially mallard, pintail, and teal, have fallen to historic lows.

By contrast, in the United Kingdom—where wild ducks may be shot in unlimited numbers, day or night, with almost any kind of shotgun, including cannons on some English estuaries—local populations of mallard, pintail, and teal are reaching historic highs. The British have no publicly paid wardens nor cumbersome resource bureaucracies. How do they do it? Through superior indoctrination with an unwritten sportsman's code of responsibility and restraint.

One afternoon I found the badly rusted remains of a peavey. It reminded me that in 1664, just as English immigrants in Virginia were starting the enormous task of clearing the virgin forest, John Evelyn published *Silva*, in which he pleaded with British landowners to plant trees to replenish the denuded countryside. "We had better be without gold than without timber," he warned. Thus began the restoration of Britain's woodlands. Tree plantings increased throughout the 1700s and early 1800s, from which time the few remaining great groves of English oak, beech, sycamore, and horse chestnut are dated.

British tree cutters were necessarily more frugal than their American counterparts. Large trees were coppiced so that multiple saplings would grow from the same rootstock, or they were pollarded, which involves cutting a tree six feet above the ground so that new shoots will be out of the reach of grazing animals. These shoots produced enormous quantities of wood for "crooks" (branches grown into natural curves for shipbuilding) and charcoal for iron smelting. It's rare to find an ancient oak in England today that wasn't pollarded, and countless country people found full-time employment in woodcraft.

Meanwhile, when American colonists weren't too exhausted from tree burning and stumping, they boasted of their wastefulness. Divorced from frugal European habits, Americans bragged about the New World's overwhelming abundance. Whereas in England, long-lived and late-maturing sturgeon had become so rare as to be reserved exclusively for royalty, in Virginia, Captain John

Smith noted, "we had more Sturgeon than could be devoured by Dog or Man." He drove in the barb by claiming that "if a Man works but three days in seven, he may get more than he can spend unless he will be exceedingly excessive . . . [and] though they fish but an hour in a day, to take more than they can eat in a week."

By the middle of the nineteenth century, Virginians had fished out their sturgeon and devastated their forests. The commonwealth began importing timber from as far west as Michigan. By 1910, the first wood began trickling in from the Pacific Northwest. Most small landowners, however, still relied on local woodlots for the oaks they adzed into sills, the splints they made into baskets, and the branches they burned for warmth. A peavey would have been a useful tool indeed.

Another oddity I found resembled a marlin spike but with a curved handle. It was one-piece, solid-cast aluminum. Because I thought of it as a marlin spike, I didn't perceive for a long time that it was a dibble used to make holes in the ground for planting bulbs and seeds. It had been cast in solid aluminum because its manufacturer had hoped that the tool would last and be used forever. That automatically dates the implement to the early 1900s, before planned obsolescence became the foundation of capitalism.

I even found an aluminum rattrap in one shed. Traps— along with scythes, pitchforks, and ax heads—were the most common tools we found in the outbuildings. Some traps were legholds for raccoons and muskrats, but most were small box traps and snapbacks for mice and rats. I began collecting the older traps. I was intrigued by the ingenuity of the different designs. Most date back to a time when Americans still believed it was possible to build a better mousetrap, and that the world would beat a path to the door of the individual who did.

At a local auction, I got into a bidding contest over an intricate woven-wire affair dating to the middle of the nineteenth century. When the bidding was done and the trap was mine, the other bidder—a museum curator, as it turned out—asked why I had put my own desire ahead of the public's interest in such artifacts. I told him that I thought most private collections of anything—be they books, insects, or mousetraps—receive better care than public collections that are all too often broken up and sold by curators more concerned with cash flow than continuity.

Before a mousetrap is added to my collection, it must catch a mouse. The simplest and still one of the most effective enclosure-type traps I have—I use it in the autumn when field mice begin to move indoors—is an antique Mason jar with a galvanized screw lid, open in the center and around which a circle of inward-pointing prongs has been soldered. If I have a "problem mouse" that is clever enough to avoid capture in other traps, the Mason jar generally does the trick.

Most of my larger traps, however, will never be tested. For example, I have an old wolf trap. Since the last local wolf was killed early in the eighteenth century, this trap will never be initiated. It hangs in an outbuilding, where black rat snakes use its edged surfaces to help shed their skins.

Although local bears survived longer than wolves—a survey team killed the last sow and her cubs in Dahl Swamp, adjoining our Cashville property, around 1951—I got my collection's bear trap from Alaska, where its relatively small size suggests it was used for black bears rather than the larger brown.

The most unusual trap I have is English, not American. It's a mantrap used to catch poachers. It works exactly like a bear trap, meaning it's difficult for one man to open by himself and impossible to escape from once one's leg is caught. Most mantraps were designed with daggerlike teeth to punish and permanently maim the trespasser. They're a testament to the power of property over personal rights, since the devices were outlawed in Britain only in the early nineteenth century. Even then they continued in unofficial use and were revived during World War I when German patrols found them to be as fiendish as British soldiers found German mustard gas.

Some of our artifacts came from an old trash pit in what is now the home pond. Although Barbara and I found numerous antique curiosities under the house—including shards of handblown glass, a large corroded copper penny, an old brass button, a belt buckle, a piece of broken crockery showing part of a coat of arms, and marble marbles from a time when some were still made of the stone that gives them their name—our most productive mine was the trash pit at the edge of the marsh near the house. If a particular style of glassware—cup, saucer, or even porcelain doll—was sold on the Eastern Shore in the 1800s, a piece of it eventually ended up there.

Although Barbara and I kept hoping we'd find something fabulously valuable, our most abundant treasures
were blue Bromo Seltzer bottles. Each was stamped
"Emerson Drug Co. Baltimore, Md.," and most included a
stock number on the bottom: 1 to 20. I now have thirty-
four of these bottles in unbroken condition and hundreds
of blue shards. Although I'm missing a few stock numbers,
a new bottle pops up at the edge of the pond every year or
two, and I'm confident that one day I'll have a complete set.

Local Indian debris sites are more specialized. Some were
devoted to making stone tools, others to making pottery,
but most to eating shellfish. One is only a hundred yards
behind the house, where a rise of land once overlooked a
spring. The spring has long since silted in, and the rise is
now part of a cultivated field. Yet the continual appearance
of flaked stone and occasionally whole implements—especially after a heavy rain following spring plowing—provides ample evidence the Indians camped there.

Find high ground next to a spring or stream anywhere
on the Eastern Shore, and you'll find Indian artifacts. Most
of the best campsites became colonial homesites. The
Indians didn't occupy the same ground year-round the way
the English settlers did, so the colonists probably didn't
think that they were doing anything wrong in building
permanent structures on temporarily abandoned camp-
grounds. There was lots of land and relatively few people,
at least by English standards. That the Indians had adapted to the environment by moving periodically to intercept
seasonal abundances never occurred to seventeenth-centu-

ry settlers, whose agriculture depended on maintaining permanently cleared properties.

The Indians showed the colonists how to construct pound nets to trap fish and how to set snares to catch game. But the Indians learned something too. They learned that it was easier to trade furs for metal than to continue making stone implements. The quality of Indian craftsmanship fell off dramatically after contact with the English. The Indians even traded furs for personal items, such as the pipes they smoked. Diagonally across the marsh and overlooking Rattrap Creek is a place where, over the years, Barbara and I and, more recently, our son, Christopher, have found dozens of broken pieces of clay pipe.

There are two types: Indian-made red pipe and English (or Dutch) white pipe. A more notable difference than color is the uniform perfection of the longer European pipe versus the stubby, even lopsided, Indian pipe. Some of the European pieces have diamond or other geometric designs on the stems, which English manufacturers or traders thought the Indians would value. In contrast, some pieces of Indian pipe show a braided but random pattern made by twisting fibers around the bowl before baking.

The European pipe is industrially perfect but culturally sterile. The Indian pipe is cruder but more personal and occasionally artistic. From the beginning, however, art and personality counted for less in the struggle for cultural dominion of the New World than industrial perfection. Even on the little hill overlooking Rattrap Creek, broken pieces of white pipe outnumber red clay pieces by better than ten to one.

This triumph of standardization is further symbolized by two items we found in the woods. One is a hickory-handled plow with a cast-iron tongue, share, and bracing bar and a steel coulter and moldboard. The other is a green enameled Virginia automobile license plate numbered "994" and dated 1912. Both were manufactured at the peak of the American Industrial Revolution, which means that both items were made to last. Even the license plate, legally valid for just a year, is fabricated of such superior steel and heavy enameling that although it was covered by dirt and vines for the better part of a century, it still came up ready for reuse.

A hundred years ago, the hickory-handled plow was state of the art. Whereas it had taken four medieval Englishmen most of one day to plow an acre of land with a span of six or eight oxen, one late nineteenth-century Virginian could plow an acre a day with only two horses pulling the hickory-handled plow. More important, whereas a good medieval English yield was half a ton of wheat per acre, by the end of the nineteenth century—thanks to the use of manure fertilizer and rotation cropping—Virginia yields were up to two tons per acre.

Then just sixty or so years ago, our Virginia farmer left his horse-drawn plow in a corner of the back field. He'd acquired a tractor, and although early tractors were mere ponies compared with modern mechanized Clydesdales, they could plow up to ten acres a day. Even better, a British genius named Harry Ferguson had invented the three-point hydraulic hitch. This not only meant that tractors

could lift their plows at the ends of fields to facilitate turning, they could also be adapted to use a variety of other
implements.

In 1989, at an auction in Craddockville, I spent
$2,300 on an old Ford tractor, a disk, and a scrape. I've
since acquired a two-bottom plow, a two-row planter, a
cultivator, a scoop, and a bush hog. After years of depend-
ing on neighbors, I'm now self-sufficient in most of my
farm chores. Although I still rent the largest part of my
arable land to Barry Lane, who rotates corn, wheat, and
soybeans, I tend about twenty acres for wildlife—using
the tractor to plow, plant, and cultivate annual crops,
mow lespedeza strips, haul logs from the woods, maintain
roads, and fill holes in the dikes. There is immense satis-
faction in accomplishing each task. Some days I can hardly wait to get through with the morning's writing and start
the tractor.

I once saw a television show in which a host asked ten
celebrity guests what they considered to be the greatest
invention of the twentieth century. Two mentioned dis-
posable razors; another, the ballpoint pen. The majority,
however, touted the airplane or the computer. No one
mentioned the three-point hitch. Yet because of the hitch,
one man can work more land more effectively today than
several hundred could a century ago. This increase in pro-
ductivity has indirectly led to a quintupling of the world's
population, which is the most significant fact of the twentieth century. Yet hardly anyone who's not a farmer has
ever heard of Harry Ferguson.

CHAPTER 9

Neighbors

Wayne Fincen, the real estate agent who sold us the farm, said that I'd like living on the Shore: "Life is easy, and you'll have little to worry about. Barbara'll mind your money, and your neighbors will mind your business."

Since Barbara keeps our accounts, she knows how little money this writer has to mind. But before we got to know

89

most of our neighbors, some of them did make up extraordinary stories about the "come-heres" on the hill.*

Even before Barbara and I took title to the farm, I
realized how easy it would be to dig out the needlerush
patch between the road and the east end of the house for
a pond. Although today it's both politically and legally
incorrect to remove a single rhizome of a wetland plant,
I'm of the opinion that marshes can be improved as well
as degraded. I see no reason that the status quo should
automatically be best, especially when I know that many
national wildlife refuges were created with bulldozers and
draglines.

The needlerush patch had already been altered, but for
the worst. In the nineteenth century, a causeway had been
built across the upper end of the marsh, which blocked the
normal ebb and flow of the tide. In the 1930s, the Works
Projects Administration ditched and straightened the formerly meandering Finney Creek for several hundred yards
above the causeway. This accelerated the flow of water to
the culvert, where floods backed up and undermined the
road's foundation. On top of that, the marsh by the house
had been used as a dump for generations. When I first
inventoried this microecosystem, I found more Norway
rats than muskrats.

---

* Our house was built on a rise of ground that, two hundred years ago, must
have been higher than today's elevation of barely ten feet above sea level. Still,
because our house is unique in the village in having a cellar, we live on the hill.
This, plus a play on my name and the German word *Reiher* (meaning
"heron"), is what led us to name the farm Heron Hill—although Heron Hope
(the latter meaning "marsh") might have been more appropriate.

Wilson Wessells and Ronnie Godwin of the Soil Conservation Service helped design the pond so that heavy rains wouldn't cause it to back onto our neighbors' properties. With the U.S. Department of Agriculture seal of approval went a $500 check that paid for the coated steel pipe and concrete block I used to build two water-control structures. (Today, I'd save many maintenance headaches by using heavy-duty plastic pipe instead of steel.) Contractor Carroll Young bulldozed much of the spoil into an island, while his father, Vincent, used an army-surplus dragline to build a dike with a sandy core to deter tunneling muskrats. Considering the circular shape of the project, the low island in the middle, and local horse-racing traditions, it was probably inevitable that someone would start the rumor that I was constructing a racetrack.

In 1970, few of my neighbors had heard of anyone digging a pond for wildlife. Irrigation ponds were the norm, and that meant stark rectangular holes with steep sides and mountains of spoil, which sometimes sat on either side of the pond for years. My circular and gradually graded excavation with an island was obviously a racecourse. Until the middle of this century, most Delmarva counties had their own fairgrounds, and many fairgrounds had their own tracks. Accomack had several where trotters and thoroughbreds competed. On a beam in the cellar of this house, near initials dating back to the 1870s, are the barely legible words: "Sunny Mae, Born March 5, 1911, One [*sic*] Silver Cup Race." The proud owner had gone down to the basement, probably to get some celebratory cider, and recorded his horse's victory.

Some neighbors imagined that I would restore Accomack's days of equine glory—except that I seemed to be putting the track in a dangerously damp spot.

"You'll have to pump it every day," one fellow warned down at the general store.

"It's a pond," I explained. "I don't intend to pump it."

"Kinda small for a racecourse," someone else observed. "More like a roller rink. The horses'll be turning from the moment they leave the gate." The men who were gathered around the stove in back chuckled at the image.

"But it's not a racecourse," I said.

"Even if you get it pumped down," a third fellow pointed out, "you're going to have trouble with mosquitoes."

"I don't plan to pump it down. I want it filled with water. It's a pond."

"If I was you," a fourth fellow suggested, "I wouldn't put it so near your house. Kids'll be sneaking in there at all hours to race trucks and motorcycles, and you'll never get any sleep."

The week after the pond was finished, a downpour filled it to overflowing. The men at the general store were so subdued that I thought they were embarrassed at having let their imaginations run wild. As I was leaving with the mail, however, one fellow came over, put his hand on my shoulder and said, "I'm sorry. We all are. You put a lot of money into that track, and it would have been good for the town."

One week in May of 1971, while Barbara stayed in New York, I spent a few days on the farm by myself, fishing for black drum in the mornings and doing chores in the afternoons. One of those chores was planting asparagus. When one neighbor saw I was alone—and standing in a trench with a shovel in my hands—he decided that Barbara was dead and I'd dug her grave. Once that theory was unleashed, a kind of logic led to the rumor that I'd killed her.

"It's for asparagus," I explained.

"Going too deep," a farmer said with more suspicion than friendly advice.

He was right, as it turned out. I smothered the asparagus roots by planting them too far down. That wasn't the problem though. When Barbara showed up two weekends later, the question some neighbors asked was, if I hadn't dug the grave for her, who had I buried there?

Before we gave up our apartment on Connecticut Avenue and moved to the Shore for good, many tales were woven about our alleged wealth. The illusion was reinforced by the fact that writers have no visible means of support. I didn't commute to an office; ergo, I must be rich enough to stay at home.

When I volunteered to read children's stories at the local radio station, the owner soon sized me up.

"You're retired military, aren't you?"

"No," I said, "although I did spend nearly five years in the navy."

"How'd you manage to retire after only five years?"

"I didn't," I said. "I'm not retired now. I'm a writer."

The station owner gave me a wink, and I knew that a new rumor was about to leave the mill: that I'd pulled the coup of the century by getting Uncle Sam to provide me with a monthly stipend, plus dental and medical benefits, after only five years of military service.

The irony of moving to the rural South, whose home-grown writers usually leave to make their marks elsewhere, is that when I lived on New York's Lower East Side in the early 1960s, I felt trapped by words. I would spend mornings in roundtable analyses of the medieval world order at Columbia, afternoons selling books in eventually every Doubleday store on Manhattan Island, and evenings helping a friend run the Pocket Theater on Third Avenue. When I complained of words, words, words, one friend took me to meet Bob Dylan and another to a loft party at Robert Rauschenberg's. More words. My mentor and former history teacher, Ben Scott Custer, who has a doctoral degree in history as well as being a retired rear admiral, urged me to try military service, where I'd find a balance between action and intellect. That's why one morning in the fall of 1963 I took the subway down to the Wall Street navy recruiting office and signed on. The service soon ferreted out my aptitude for words and offered to send me to language school. Unhappily for the nation, but happily for me, the relevance of my learning Vietnamese grew with each passing week. I spent my first tour in Saigon administering a translation division and my second tour with the Rand Corporation interrogating—excuse me, the euphemism was "interviewing"—prisoners of war.

When I take a summer's day away from the writing board now, it's usually to launch my Boston Whaler well before the rest of the Shore is awake. Each time I run

through the inlet, I shed old intellectual skin. I'm sometimes ten miles out before the stars begin to fade, and I
have occasionally caught a fish even before the sun cleared
the horizon. Numbers, not words, bracket my time at sea.
Compass points and fathoms matter, not whether a man at
a bus stop is concealing a revolver (*súng lục*) or merely the
fact he's rich (*súng tục*).

Two things I brought back from Vietnam were an abiding
distrust of authority and a keen respect for the savvy of
some local police chiefs. When Barbara and I were still
commuting from New York, the farmhouse was robbed
twice. The first time, Sheriff Adair Matthews looked over
the list of stolen items and concluded the thieves were
white.

"How do you know?" I asked.

"Blacks won't take another man's fishing tackle."

The sheriff soon caught the culprit—a white man—
who picked up a partner while in jail. The team returned
the first night after the leader got out on probation in
exchange for his guilty plea. This time he took pillowcas-
es off the beds and used them as sacks to carry away my
decoy collection. Since stealing hand-carved decoys is the
same as taking any other easily identifiable art object, the
sheriff and I soon tracked down the stolen birds in
Maryland and New York. This time the instigating thief
was sentenced to eight years, which meant that he was
out in less than three.

Not long after he was freed, I ran into the sheriff who
told me the thief was up to his old tricks. "Don't worry

though," the sheriff added. "You scared him off the seaside. He's working the bayside now. We'll soon have him back behind bars. The hard part is keeping him there."

Burglary wasn't the only abuse we suffered during the commuter phase of our move to the Shore. One spring weekend we came down to see that poachers had left spent shotgun shells on the dike near the house, and I found dead wooducks floating in the pond. At a party that May, a neighbor boasted that his son had killed three pheasants in our lower yard without even leaving his vehicle. Even more serious was the squatter who was evicted from the house on the second piece of property we purchased and returned one night to burn the place down.

The sheriff and I both knew who did it. "But you can't prove anything," he said, "and she doesn't have any money, even if you could. Just file an insurance claim and forget it." The only trouble was, we didn't have insurance.

At times, I got the impression that some "born-heres" thought they could say or do anything without hurting our feelings, since they believed that "come-heres" have no feelings to hurt. The winter after we bought the farm, we were invited to what we were told was the social highlight of the Christmas season by someone hoping to supervise our farmhouse's restoration. We left Manhattan early Friday afternoon but didn't reach our host's home until the party was well under way that evening. While Barbara went to find someplace to put our coats, I went to get drinks in the kitchen. On the way there, I was intercepted by a woman who was apparently auditioning for a role in a Tennessee Williams play.

"In high school," she told me, "Mary Lou was the pretty one. *I* was the plain one, and *she* was the pretty one. Well, look who's the pretty one *now*." She batted her lashes and thrust up her décolletage.

"Hmm," I acknowledged and sidled by to the kitchen. I was soon joined by a surly chap whose eyes were so close together that I thought he might be a cyclops.

"What'ja doin' with my woman?" he asked.

"What woman?" I said.

The question inflamed him.

"Your name's Reegur, Rugur, sompin' like that," he said. "German, hain't it?"

"Reiger," I corrected. "It rhymes with Geiger. Of German extraction, yes."

"Well, listen heah, Rye-gur," he said. "We beat the Germans in two wars, and we can do it again."

"I don't doubt it," I concurred. "Germany is still a divided nation [true at the time], with neither the resources nor the will to wage war against anybody."

The man's jaw dropped. Was I implying that I was 'merican like him?

I left the kitchen, found Barbara, and told her what had happened. Without a word, she retrieved our coats and we left.

That was the dark side of buying cheap land on the Shore a quarter century ago. It went with the billboard that stood just north of the Owl Restaurant on Route 13—a huge American flag topped by the words "Stand Up for America" and captioned by "Join the KKK."

That sign is long gone, along with many of the uglier attitudes it embodied. Increased suburbanization has adversely affected several local ecosystems, but it has also diluted some of the area's more sinister social traditions. Barbara and I are no longer regarded as quite so alien, since we've shared the communal rites of raising a child on the Shore. We—especially Barbara—are integrated in local activities ranging from fund-raising for the Eastern Shore Public Library to preventing a major residential development on Cedar Island between Locustville and the sea.

We've also been here long enough so that far-flung readers can track me down. One day a young man appeared who had walked all the way from New Orleans, where his application to the Jesuit Order had been rejected. He'd come to persuade me to meet Carl Sagan and Ronald Reagan to solve the world's problems. The wanderer showed me a manuscript that he said was the key to everything. He camped in the woods down the road for two days while my anxious wife fed him and I tried to decipher what he'd written. It was hopeless, and after I told him so, he decided to move on in search of Dr. Sagan.

Two years later, the wanderer wrote to us from a Michigan penitentiary. He'd done something to get arrested so he'd have a roof over his head and three meals a day while finishing his masterwork. The trouble was, he said, the work was done, but the warden wouldn't let him go. Could I help?

CHAPTER 10

Guests

Perhaps it was getting married or reaching thirty. Maybe it was having our apartment robbed three times in two years and having to deal with New York's jaded police, who wouldn't even come to inventory our losses. Whatever it was, Barbara and I lost much of our enthusiasm for the city after acquiring the farm. Although we went to the Manhattan premiere of Dale Bell's movie *Woodstock*, we passed on his invitation to meet the Who. (What would we talk about?) At the same time, many of our New York friends seemed out of place when they visit-ed Virginia. Only the fact that local people didn't know the smell of marijuana saved several guests from being arrested as they rocked, giggled, and inhaled on the veranda of the old Wachapreague Inn.

One film star enjoyed poking around the many general stores we still had on the Shore and where his bell-bottom trousers and shoulder-length hair attracted considerable attention. He especially liked it when proprietors asked him, "May I help you, sir? Or is it, 'madam?' "

After we moved to Washington in 1971, we made new friends among the bureaucratic bourgeoisie of the conser-vation community. Our farm soon became an unofficial field station for the Smithsonian Institution. Marine mam-malogists Jim Mead and Charley Potter sometimes left dead whales and dolphins in our backyard so maggots would clean the bones. If a neighbor asked about the odor, we offered to show him or her what we had, but only the Corsons came, and they were as delighted as we were by the halo of flies attracted to the carcasses, which in turn attracted a wonderful variety of birds.

Once, when Jim and Charley couldn't contact us before setting out from Washington, they asked a herpetologist to come along and help. By the time they arrived, we were back—and a good thing, too. When the herpetologist saw how much bloody labor was involved in wrestling a seven-teen-foot baby finback off a sandbar with a sixteen-foot

Boston Whaler, towing the beast to a launch ramp, winching it onto a truck, driving the truck to our farm, picking a spot in the garden where we hoped to grow pumpkin-sized tomatoes the following spring, and carving the creature into its component parts so that Jim and Charley could take them back to Washington, the herpetologist explained that he was, after all, a reptile specialist and not up to dissecting whales.

Instead, he smiled at my anecdotes about water snakes and snapping turtles in the estuary, and my observation that diamondback terrapin were so abundant in our seaside marshes that one could find them by the hundreds in the spring when they crawled up on the banks of local tidal creeks to breed. The specialist pointed out that freshwater snakes and turtles cannot tolerate submersion in salt water; therefore, I could not possibly catch water snakes in minnow traps kept in a tidal creek or see snapping turtles feeding on fish carcasses dumped from the road into the same tidal stream. As for my fantasy of countless diamondback terrapin in Virginia's seaside marshes, he'd be happy to send me copies of articles published in the 1930s documenting the terrapin's decline. Diamondbacks, he assured me, were an endangered species, if not actually extinct.

By contrast, when Roger Conant—author of the *Peterson Field Guide to Reptiles and Amphibians*—visited the Shore, he was well past the popularly assumed age of retirement but neither too old nor too concerned about appearances to keep from charging through the underbrush in pursuit of an escaping king snake. He flung himself on it, brought it up between his knees so that he could catch the neck just behind the head, and then proclaimed that at that moment, the king snake was the most beautiful creature on earth. Later, when I suggested that the range map in his book regarding the distribution of the broad-headed skink should be modified to include the Eastern Shore of Virginia, he was neither defensive nor patronizing. He asked only for more details and, if possible, a confirming photograph. If the change has not yet been made, it's because publishers are sometimes more concerned with cost than with accuracy.

Like all exceptional scientists, Charley Potter has more than one specialty. He began his research career with rodents, and in the winter of 1976 he made several trips to our farm to help run a trapline to gather sufficient samples to learn whether Accomack's black-furred muskrats represent a distinct subspecies or are merely a racial variant of the predominantly brown-furred *Ondatra zibethica*. The evolution of new species from peripheral isolates through a process biologists call allopathic speciation is common among rodents. Muskrats in Newfoundland, for example, are now considered a separate species: *Ondatra obscura*.

The skulls and other evidence that Charley and I collected led to his conclusion that Accomack's muskrats are only a racial variant. During our work together we exchanged reminiscences of other traplines and trails and our hope that high fur prices—then up to $9 for a prime black muskrat and $25 for a big raccoon —would not only provide supplemental income for seasonally unemployed watermen and help control two prolific species with few natural enemies but also provide the carrot for wetlands protection that the stick of federal legislation lacked.

Although the price of farmland had risen steadily from $200 an acre in 1970 to more than $1000 by the time of Charley's muskrat research, an acre of salt marsh could still be bought for under $50 in 1976. In Virginia, that included (and still does) title down to mean low water. Yet even at $50 an acre, who wants to pay annual taxes on wetlands unless there's some profit or pleasure in it?

Until the early 1980s, shellfishing, duck hunting, and trapping were traditional sources of such pleasure and profit. Today, however, wildfowl and shellfish are declining and/or contaminated, and animal-rights zealots have achieved through intimidation what they never won in the courts. The fur industry is moribund because people fear being assaulted for wearing real fur coats. I still trap raccoons and occasionally muskrats to keep their numbers in check, but I can no longer defray the taxes I pay on the marsh where many of these animals are found by selling their skins. Unless I find someone to take the meat, I leave the carcasses on the field behind the house for turkey vultures, black vultures, young redtail hawks, and an occasional bald eagle to scavenge. (A visitor said the circling flocks reminded him of Africa.)

Is it any wonder that wetlands owners are an increasingly frustrated part of the land-rights movement? Why should we have to pay taxes on property that we can no longer profit from in any way? Wouldn't it be more sensible to restore the fur industry and reverse the decline of

ducks and shellfish than to create laws that prohibit taxpayers from doing anything more with their wetlands than
a trespasser could?

In 1935, an English ecologist named Charles Elton
observed that the composition of all wildlife communities
is dictated by food chains. The niche that any animal occu-
pies is determined by what it eats and what eats it.
Protecting individual animals is meaningless unless you
also protect their niches. And if you protect their niches,
you won't have to worry about protecting individual animals. Most niches can sustain a high turnover of individuals yet continue to support the species.*

Wildlife sentimentalists ignore this fact of life. It inter-
feres with their fantasy that the wren or cardinal they see at
the feeder this fall is the same bird they've seen for years.

---

* In recent years, some ecologists have begun mocking the niche concept in
order to undermine the validity of traditional fish and wildlife management or
to stop the creation and introduction of genetically engineered organisms. At
a conference organized by the American Society of Microbiology in June
1985, ecologist Philip J. Regal of the University of Minnesota remarked,
"Most ecologists don't refer to niches any more. . . . It is really an antiquated
concept. There is no reason at this point to believe a species is so highly per-
fected that nothing else can replace it."

Such scorn also underpins the notion of "ecosystem management," a good
idea in that it encourages biological specialists to look at an entire ecosystem
before taking steps that might adversely impact it, but bad in that—carried to
its logical extreme—ecosystem management inhibits biologists from taking
any steps at all. The reality of ecosystem management is that it has divorced
the scientist from the practical worlds of the forester, farmer, and fisherman,
and it provides animal rightists with a scientific rationale, ultimately turning
the phrase "ecosystem management" into an oxymoron that lends new, ironic
meaning to another oxymoron: political science.

What they're seeing, of course, is the same niche, year after year, with an ever-changing guard of feathered actors playing the same evolutionarily assigned roles. As each individual actor is carried offstage by disease or predation, another wren or cardinal soon takes its place. And since the appearance and behavior of Wren Number 2, 22, or 222 are the same as those of Wren Number 1, the sentimentalist insists that it's still "Walter" or "Winnie."

In the spring of 1978, Charley Potter and ornithologist John Barber came to the farm to collect birds to replace the moth-eaten specimens on display in the Smithsonian's Birds of the District of Columbia Region exhibit on the ground floor of the Natural History Museum. John and Charley drove the four hours from Washington because, with suburbanization and sentimentality rippling out from the city, it was impossible to collect birds anywhere nearer the District of Columbia region.

Yet even Barbara hesitated to allow them to shoot songbirds. She's perfectly content for me to bring in dove, quail, duck, geese, even blackbirds and starlings, because we eat all I shoot. Barbara accepts my credo that if it dies, it also fries. For that reason, she saw little point in killing songbirds, since John and Charley weren't going to eat them. She also worried that some of the songbirds they shot would not be replaced. I thought she was worried about woodpeckers, but she was really anxious about the one species I was absolutely certain would immediately replace itself: the mockingbird.

"You're not going to let John or Charley kill Caruso, are you?" she asked.

"Who's Caruso?"

"My mockingbird."

"If they need a mockingbird for the exhibit, I'd be happy to see Caruso move to Washington. He kept me awake half the night."

"Caruso is no ordinary mockingbird. He sings to me when I'm working outside."

"If he does, it's because he sees you as a rival."

"If John or Charley shoots Caruso, I'll put a powerful laxative into everything you eat for three months running!"

Her poor pun aside, she clearly meant business, so I went to find Charley to tell him to cool it on the mockingbird.

"Where's John?" I asked.

"He just got a fox sparrow; he's after a thrasher. He'll be back soon."

"Be sure to tell him about the mockingbird, okay?"

"Right."

Charley is a man of many qualities, but he's not an effective message center. Barbara was reorganizing her spice shelf when John returned with a brown thrasher. He showed her the bird, then held out a "bonus" he'd killed in the lilacs. The mockingbird had a wad of cotton stuffed in its mandibles to prevent blood from soiling its feathers. John innocently pointed out that the only perceptible damage was a shot-clipped primary feather, which wouldn't even show once the specimen was freeze-dried in a perched position.

I heard Barbara shriek and came running. I opened the door just as John burst through with a can of cinnamon right behind.

"Get out of here, you murderers!" Barbara yelled. I heard the can thunk off John's skull. Charley came in the back door in time to get a jar of sage in the chest. We fled.

"Hope this doesn't get you into any trouble," said Charley as he began backing his Volkswagen bus down the driveway.

"Send us our clothes and dop kits!" John called.

They were gone in a cloud of clamshell dust. When I went in the house, Barbara was sitting at the kitchen table with tears in her eyes. "You let them shoot Caruso," she said.

I was going to try to explain again about niches, but said instead, "I'm sorry."

The next day, three mockingbirds fought for control of the garden. Within a week, the victor was singing from every vantage point between the garage and the pecan grove. Although Barbara spent a lot of time in the garden that spring while the new mockingbird sang cardinal and vireo medleys, she was neither impressed nor appeased.

"The new mockingbird sings as well—and as endlessly," I pointed out, "as his predecessor."

"No, he doesn't. No bird sings as well as Caruso did."

That fall, a friend with the U.S. Fish and Wildlife Service and I strung a mist net down the dike, parallel to a row of autumn olive and multiflora rose shrubs. We caught, banded, and released dozens of passerines, including a mockingbird, but not the one by the house. Thus, I'm not sure whether it was Caruso's replacement or another that finally melted Barbara's reserve the next spring.

The breeding season had come both early and late. Many insect- and fish-eating birds had drifted north on the warming winds of March but were left without food by the chilling winds of April. An osprey that couldn't find any fish in the estuary visited our pond several times a day to snatch largemouth bass and bluegill from the warm surface waters. The bird carried his booty off to the northeast, where his mate was occupied with egg-laying. Sometimes within an hour, the osprey would herald his return with the distinctive cry of his species.

Several days after the osprey first appeared, Barbara came into my office. "I've decided the new mockingbird is better than Caruso," she said.

Jolted from somewhere far away, I could only say, "Huh?"

"You remember when your friends from the Smithsonian murdered Caruso?" (A vision of lab technicians in white coats gunning down the famous opera star flickered through my brain.) "Well, his successor can do something Caruso couldn't do."

"What's that?"

"Imitate ospreys."

Now that *did* interest me. Sure enough, just as I reached the kitchen door, I heard an osprey.

"Fantastic!" I exclaimed.

"Idiot," said Barbara. "That's the real bird. See him? Wait a bit."

The osprey hovered, stooped, but at the last moment pulled up, calling as he did.

"Listen to him," I remarked, "blaming everyone but himself."

"Now who's anthropomorphizing!"

"I'm not," I replied. "I'm merely using the language of human emotion to confirm a scientific observation."

Barbara smiled.

"At least I don't give wild creatures Christian names," I said.

"Well, I do, and the osprey is George, because of what you just said."

On his next attempt, "George" grabbed a big bluegill and flapped off to the northeast. Before he'd quite disappeared, a waterfall of bird song tumbled from the chimney top. The mockingbird sang a blend of white-throated sparrow, red-winged blackbird, and bobwhite quail songs interspersed with the usual mockingbird prattle. After nearly a minute of uninterrupted melody, I thought I heard the cry of an osprey high overhead and behind me. I whirled around, expecting to see the fish hawk, but there was nothing. I turned back in time to see the mockingbird's mandibles move as it made the sound again.

"Amazing!"

"I told you so," said Barbara. "This bird is even better than Caruso."

Exasperated, I tried once again to explain: "Caruso and this bird are the same species with the same intrinsic capacity for mimicry. Caruso could have imitated an osprey if he'd ever heard one."

"Yes, and you'll be telling me next all about niches."

"Exactly! Mockingbirds imitate what they hear. They pick up the sounds of whatever other birds share their niche. For this particular mockingbird in this particular place and season, it happens to be an osprey."

"You just won't accept the fact that Pavarotti is a better singer than Caruso."

"Pavarotti?"

"Yes. Didn't I say? That's the new bird's name."

CHAPTER 11

Birding

N ot long ago, I was driving down Route 13 when a car went flying by with one of those rather-be bumper stickers on the back. You know the kind: "I'd Rather Be Sailing" or "I'd Rather Be Skiing." This bumper sticker said, "I'd Rather Be Birding." I was dumbfounded. Birding is the only recreation—other than listening to the car radio or a tape—you can do while driving. On Eastern Shore stretches of Route 13, I've seen bald eagles in aerial courtship, kestrels catching crickets and mice, and legions of wintering wildfowl settling into roadside fields. Did the driver of the bumper-stickered car really imagine that birding is done only at selected times and places? Was he or she really unable to see the sky for the highway?

Birding is like religion: Some people enjoy ritual and group participation; others prefer privacy. For me, birding is as intensely personal as writing, and just as I shy away from the word *author*, I'm uncomfortable being known as a *birder*. I winced when reviewer Phoebe-Lou Adams categorized me as "primarily a bird watcher" in *The Atlantic Monthly*, because it seemed to diminish my interest in all the rest of nature.

Birding is something I do unconsciously whenever I step outdoors. Since we moved to the farm, I don't even have to step outdoors to get my feathered fix. Our kitchen window overlooks the pond and provides an ever-changing panorama of waterbirds. At different times, I've seen every species of heron here except the reddish egret. In late summer, postbreeding flocks of snowy and great egrets sometimes mantle the pond's bordering trees so that it looks like Christmas in August. Canada geese are with us year-round, but in winter, they're occasionally joined by snow geese, a stray blue, and even a white-front or two. One autumn, I trapped and banded dozens of blackducks, mallards, woodducks, hooded mergansers, and a hen ring-necked duck thirty yards from the kitchen window. Other waterfowl regulars include gadwall, blue- and green-winged teal, and bufflehead. Less regular visitors are pintail (including a drake to the sunflower feeder [!] in January 1994), American wigeon (also a drake Eurasian wigeon one week in 1975), shovelers, ruddy ducks, lesser and greater scaup, redheads, and common goldeneye. Before their numbers shrank, coot and canvasback came as well. Today, some of my hunting visitors find it hard to believe I took the picture of the canvasbacks in *The Wings of Dawn* just outside the kitchen window or that the flying flocks of pintail and wigeon were photographed on the dike across the pond.

I normally don't report unusual birds on the pond, because I don't want our home to be overrun with obsessive-compulsive strangers. For example, an immature white-fronted goose showed up one day in April 1994, and the only person who heard about it was Gary Costanzo, the commonwealth's waterfowl biologist. Likewise, a pair of ring-necked ducks stayed well into May that spring, but only Gary and I speculated whether they would attempt to nest this far south. But one unusual sighting almost got out of hand on May 19th. Gary and his assistant, Donald Hayes, were on the Shore that day to check woodduck nesting boxes, so they were able to provide credentialed confirmation of the fact that the two black-bellied whistling ducks mixed in with the mallards and Canada geese on the pond were unbanded, untoe-clipped, and free-flying, hence, bona fide wild birds and not somebody's escaped pets. Word got out the way it does among birders, and soon my phone was ringing with inquiries from as far away as Richmond and Pittsburgh about where, exactly, Locustville was and how soon after dawn would visitors be allowed to see the ducks. Fortunately, we avoided having to hire an off-duty deputy from the sheriff's department to direct traffic, because the whistling ducks finally departed.

During a mild January week in the otherwise harsh winter of 1993–94, a coot showed up for the first time in many years. With its large white beak stuck on a little black head, its long legs and oversized feet, the coot was like a clown chicken as it scampered over the lawn, pecking and scavenging the less well digested fecal slugs of nearly a hundred geese. The "mud hen" also tried to referee every goosey squabble. It bobbed back and forth between the feather-pulling Canadas, always on the side of the overdog. When a fight stopped as abruptly as it had started, the coot would go back to scavenging the droppings of the grazing geese. Once, one squabble triggered another forty yards away. The coot was perplexed. It dashed toward one fray, then took off running to the other, weaving among the many onlookers. It almost got to the second fight when it suddenly remembered something it had forgotten to do at the first. Back it dashed, but not before the geese abruptly settled down. The coot was like an incompetent sheepherder, always trying to keep its charges under control, but never quite succeeding.

Pied-billed grebes also appear in the pond, and I keep hoping that a pair will nest here. Birds I'm not happy to see, however—especially since I'm seeing more and more of them—are double-crested cormorants. They're as efficient at catching white perch and largemouth bass as otters, but since the otters can't fly elsewhere to feed, I'd rather they have the exclusive fishing rights here.

Although it's not a large pond, its location at the head of an estuary explains why we're also visited by such unlikely species as the common loon (once); mute and tundra swans (once each); yellowlegs (commonly); willets (so common that they used to breed on the dike and still breed across the road); a variety of terns, including the Caspian (twice); and occasional black skimmers on extremely high tides.

Gulls use the pond as a rest stop, going and coming from the fields. On my birthday in 1976, I found a dead laughing gull in perfect breeding plumage floating in the pond. I mounted the bird with arched wings on a drift-wood board facing a male fiddler crab with raised cheliped. Not many years ago, I gave most of my best mounts, including the laughing gull, to the Cape Charles National Wildlife Refuge, where some are now on display in the visitors' center.

I'm astonished when I meet someone with a reputation as an outdoors enthusiast who knows little about birds. Observing bird behavior is not only intellectually satisfying, it can sometimes spell the difference between an outing's success or failure. When I'm offshore fishing, for example, I like seeing storm-petrels, but I prefer seeing shearwaters. This is because storm-petrels feed primarily on plankton, while shearwaters feed on squid and small fish pushed to the surface by larger fish—meaning game-fish. Storm-petrels may indicate a fertile setting, but shear-waters tell you that what you're after is actually there beneath the waves.

My favorite offshore telltale species is the sandwich tern. It's not a better indicator of gamefish than the Cory's and greater shearwaters that I regularly see off Virginia, or the Audubon's shearwaters that I occasionally see, but its behavior is easier to interpret. Sandwich terns regularly forage many miles from the barrier islands where they breed. While traveling to and from the fishing grounds, they fly well above the water. But when they're tracking game, anticipating big fish to push little ones up, they course low over the surface and turn every which way the big fish turn.

One June morning—when substantial runs of small bluefin tuna were still found off Virginia, and for that matter, we still had large breeding colonies of crested terns, because we also still had large schools of sand eels to support them—I took a conservation colleague out in my Boston Whaler. By 8 A.M., neither we nor the rest of the trolling fleet had seen any action. I then spied a pair of sandwich terns coursing low over the calm surface some distance away. Sheldon Kinsel thought I'd lost my mind when I took off in hot pursuit, with the lures jumping and cartwheeling in the wake.

When I tried a shortcut and zigged, the birds zagged. When I zagged, they zigged. Although I never quite lost sight of them, I never got closer than a hundred yards. After running more than two miles from the other boats, I decided the situation was hopeless. I slowed, turned, and began to troll back. At that moment, the birds turned and came our way. Just before they crossed our wake, I shouted, "Watch this!" in the happy certainty that comes with having seen it before. The water exploded beneath each bird, and two reels screamed. Half an hour later, the tails of a matched pair of fifty-five-pound bluefin tuna stuck out of the ice chest in front of the center console. It pays to know your birds.

A similarly pragmatic perspective underlies my management of nesting boxes around the farm. The very idea of building birdhouses, nailing them to trees, and forgetting about them distresses me as much as the thought of fish traps lost in the ocean that continue to attract and kill fish until the traps fall apart—which often takes many years. Putting up a birdhouse is easy; putting it up where it's protected, productive, and easily maintained requires some knowledge of the birds themselves.

I relocated my purple martin houses after learning what these birds eat. Martin aficionados (and the manufacturers of martin houses) advertise that martins eat their weight in mosquitoes every day. That claim has never made much sense to me since diurnal martins spend much of their flying time high in the air, while crepuscular mosquitoes hunt close to the ground for warm-blooded prey. Only recently, however, have researchers found that fully one-third of the martins' summer diet—and in some areas nearly 100 percent—is composed of such bona fide mosquito-eaters as damselflies and dragonflies. Another large percentage of the birds' diet includes beneficial honeybees.

I enjoy the cheerful chatter of martins and decided to move their nesting condos somewhere that would be beneficial to both of us. The bend of the dike across the road and next to the marsh is ideal. Since biting greenhead flies are ferocious inhabitants of every healthy tidal marsh, and since 16 percent of the martins' diet elsewhere is composed of flies, I like to think that the local nesting martins' diet now approaches 100 percent greenheads. Meanwhile, the martin houses are now well away from the home pond where the mosquito-eating dragonflies and damselflies are active.

Tree swallows eat mosquitoes because the birds nest closer to the damp ground where mosquitoes breed. I've increased the swallows' odds of encountering mosquitoes by putting up most of their nesting boxes on one-inch galvanized pipes (to deter climbing black snakes) and within six feet of the ground. These boxes are not actually made for tree swallows. They're bluebird boxes from Bailey, North Carolina, but they work equally well for tree swallows and are wonderfully easy to maintain.

The top is metal-sheathed for added years of service, and the entrance hole is metal-sheathed to prevent starlings from converting the box into a nesting cavity for themselves. Because the front of each box is hinged for quick cleaning, I can remove the old nest as soon as a brood fledges. First, however, I inspect the nest for blowfly pupae. If a nest cup is infested with this bloodsucking parasite, I dust the interior of the box with a one-half percent mixture of rotenone powder. If mud daubers or paper wasps have built nests, I use an aerosol spray containing pyrethrin to kill the insects.

With such simple management, I frequently get a second and occasionally a third brood from each box before the summer ends. First broods are almost all tree swallows. Second broods are about two-thirds tree swallows and one-third bluebirds, with two-thirds of the nesting boxes being used. The final nesting usually involves fewer than ten boxes, but almost all house a bluebird family. Without regular maintenance, I'd have little bluebird production since this species is territorially less aggressive than the tree swallow.

So long as tree swallows and bluebirds do well here, I know that other birds nesting in my hedges and grassy filter strips—field, song, and chipping sparrows; goldfinches; thrashers; wrens; meadowlarks; kingbirds; and quail—are also doing well. Nesting boxes can be excellent environmental indicators, but they must be regularly maintained to serve as such. One spring, after the wheat was aerially sprayed with malathion, I found one or both adult tree swallows dead in every nesting box. Beneath them were cold eggs or dead nestlings. The birds had been poisoned by the contaminated insects they'd fed on. That summer, I noticed a comparable decline in quail broods, since quail chicks are highly dependent on insects during the first few weeks of their lives.

I've since banned aerial spraying anywhere on the farm for any reason. If the ground is too wet for the farmer to get his applicator onto the fields, sorry about that—no exceptions. Ironically, the money saved by not aerially spraying sometimes offsets the money lost to insect pests, especially if the harvest is only a week or two away. Since the farmer knows that I receive nearly as much money from leasing hunting rights as I receive from him in cropland rents, he has come to accept the concept that quail yield is as important to me as wheat yield is to him.

My pragmatic view of birds doesn't diminish my wonder for their many complex behaviors. Having free-flying Canada geese on the farm year-round—being able to observe the pairs that raise their young on my ponds each spring—has convinced me that each goose knows every other goose individually. In winter, when resident geese may range far from here, they rejoice in reunions. Many also come to know me as an individual, and I can walk among them while they graze, whereas a stranger may cause them to fly away. It's not my clothing they recognize, for I don't always wear the same clothes. They do get nervous when I crouch, however. Even the kind of crouch matters. When I stoop and pretend to pick grass, the birds just watch. But when I crouch as if to stalk them, the birds begin talking and walk away. If I actually begin to crawl toward them, the geese quickly get airborne.

One key to successful hunting is to freeze when you see game. Tell the average hunter to freeze, however, and he'll crouch. Birds see this movement and then note the predatory posture. I like to demonstrate the importance of stillness in hunting (or birding) when flocks of geese are flying from our fields to the estuary in the late afternoon. I tell friends to remain motionless, no matter how exposed, as the first flock approaches. The birds make no special effort to rise out of range. When a second flock comes, I tell my companions to crouch, and they see for themselves how the flock opens and the birds strain for altitude.

When someone shoots a resident goose, survivors of the flock seem to hold me responsible. They become more wary of me, and their conversations on the lawn are far less relaxed when I'm about. By spring, however, their need to get on with life triggers, if not forgiveness, then forgetfulness. By the end of the summer, proud parent geese will allow me to inspect their broods.

Just as young married people fall into two categories—those with children and those without, whose attitudes and behaviors differ according to their respective group—that's also true of geese. Parent geese march their offspring around the farm, showing them where all the ponds are. The ideal pond has submerged aquatic vegetation and ample grass around the margins for food, and no trees nearby that could harbor hawks and owls. It also has few turtles and largemouth bass that might eat the smaller goslings and an island where the birds can bed down safely from foxes. Since the pond that comes closest to providing all these benefits is in the upper field, that's where the geese with young goslings spend most of their time.

In the process of marching around the farm, the geese lose many offspring unable to withstand the rigors of gosling boot camp. Among birds parenting for the first time, these losses may be a hundred percent. When that happens, the adults also lose the status that goes with being a parent, and they're exiled to one of the "gosling-less ponds" where they'll spend the summer. Meanwhile, successful parents establish nurseries where young are loosely creched and looked after by all the adults. If geese without offspring turn up, they're quickly driven away by parent geese who'll tolerate the proximity of other mature birds only so long as they're escorting young.

Although the idea is anathema to scientists, some birds are so individual they have what amounts to personality. That may happen even among birds not as long-lived as geese. Several years ago, I contributed a monograph on "Eastern Screech Owl Nesting and Feeding in Accomack County" to *The Raven* (vol. 63, no. 2), published by the Virginia Society of Ornithology. I observed that an owl's diet depends not only on where it nests and/or roosts, but possibly on the taste of the individual bird. One male screech owl near the village of Daughtery, for example, regularly supplied his mate and young with starlings and mice, while another male with a brood only two hundred yards away appeared to prefer warblers.

Also, from the evidence of pellets and food remains found in nesting boxes, screech owls in the Finney and Rattrap Creek swamps eat crayfish and frogs as well as occasional songbirds. They snip off the crayfish heads and claws just as humans do to eat such crustaceans. Several species of frog are also eaten; the most common found in Accomack boxes is the southern leopard frog. Although American and Fowler's toads are common throughout the county, we found no evidence that screech owls prey on them.

Screech owls are sometimes characterized as "feathered wildcats" because of their ability to kill creatures larger or more feisty than themselves. At least one screech owl that roosts along Finney Creek lives up to that reputation. In addition to the usual assortment of cardinal beaks, bluejay feathers, and woodpecker legs we find at most screech owl roosting sites, this screech owl has successfully killed a half-grown rabbit and a weasel.

A weasel is no small undertaking for a raptor of any size. Records exist of a European buzzard being over-whelmed by a weasel and of a golden eagle barely surviving a similar encounter. An Accomack neighbor, Steve Van Kesteren, remembers a domestic gobbler turkey on his farm being killed by an ambitious weasel weighing only a tiny fraction of his forty-pound bird. For a screech owl to take on a weasel requires either a blissful ignorance of that animal's capacity for self-defense or a fecklessness to match the weasel's own.

CHAPTER 12

The Bird Count

Omorning in the spring of 1972, while Barbara
and I were working in the lower yard, we noticed a
car with Ohio plates passing back and forth on the road.
On the fourth pass, the driver pulled in and asked, "Is there
a cemetery around here? There's one shown on my topo
map, but I can't find it." When we pointed to the cemetery

behind us, the driver looked disappointed. "I imagined it
would be larger." Then he gamely added, "Do you mind if
I bird there? Cemeteries are great places for birds!"

That's how we met Jim Bruce, who'd come to the Shore
to add species to his life list that he could never hope to see
in Ohio. As we talked and he realized that I shared his
interest in birds, he proposed we initiate a Christmas Bird
Count in Locustville. "The peninsula is narrow enough
here," he said, "we could design a count circle including a
little of both the Chesapeake and the Atlantic. Counters
could see anything from a brown-headed nuthatch to a
gannet."

The first Christmas Bird Count came into being after
Frank M. Chapman, Jr., the editor of *Bird-Lore*, proposed
in the 1900 edition (p. 192):

> It is not many years ago that sportsmen were accus-
> tomed to meet on Christmas Day, "choose sides,"
> and then, as representatives of the two bands result-
> ing, hie them to the fields and woods on the cheer-
> ful mission of killing practically everything in fur or
> feathers that crossed their path—if they could. These
> exceptional opportunities for winning the laurels of
> the chase were termed "side hunts," and reports of
> the hundreds of non-game birds which were some-
> times slaughtered during a single hunt were often
> published in our leading sportsmen's journals, with
> perhaps a word of editorial commendation for the
> winning side. We are not certain that the side hunt is
> wholly a thing of the past, but we feel assured that no

reputable sportsman's journal of today would venture to publish an account of one, unless it were to condemn it; and this very radical change of tone is one of the significant signs of the times.

Now *Bird-Lore* proposes a new kind of Christmas side hunt in the form of a Christmas bird census, and we hope that all our readers who have the opportunity will aid us in making it a success by spending a portion of Christmas Day with the birds and sending a report of their "hunt" to *Bird-Lore* before they retire that night. Such reports should be headed by the locality, hour of starting and returning, character of the weather, direction and force of the wind, and the temperature, the latter taken when starting. The birds observed should then be added following the order in which they are given by the A.O.U. [American Ornithological Union] "Check List," with, if possible, the exact or approximate number of individuals of each species observed.

Nearly a century later, the ground rules for Chapman's Christmas bird census are not only little changed but are regarded by compilers with a reverence reserved for Holy Writ. What has changed are the levels of participation and reported bird observations. On the first Christmas Count in 1900, twenty-seven people counted birds in twenty-five localities. By 1994, more than 43,000 people were counting birds in more than 1,668 localities.

In 1900, Pacific Grove, California, was tops with thirty-six species, while Chapman himself saw only eighteen species near his home in Englewood, New Jersey. In Pacific Grove today (now included in the Monterey Peninsula count), more than sixty participants may count up to 175 species for one of the highest counts in the nation. (Moss Landing and Morro Bay, California; Corpus Christi and Freeport, Texas; and Cocoa, Florida, often have over two hundred species each.) But even Englewood, New Jersey (now part of the Hackensack-Ridgewood count) may have up to seventy observers who see as many as ninety-two species—not bad for a suburb of New York City.

Thus inspired, Jim Bruce, neighbor Anne Corson, Barbara, and I initiated the Wachapreague Christmas Bird Count. It is called that even though the center of the count circle lies a little west of Locustville. Over the past two decades, the count has grown in reputation, thanks largely to a small but reliable contingent of ringers who spot the majority of the 130-plus species we sometimes tally. What distinguishes our count from the Chincoteague and Cape Charles counts to the north and south is that the majority of our participants are local residents and rank amateurs.

Our count's prime directive calls for enthusiasm, not expertise. From the outset, we conceived of the count more as a learning experience for the many rather than a stellar opportunity for the few. Nationally ranked birders Harry Armistead and Charlie Vaughn spend as much time helping their less-skilled companions distinguish one sparrow from another as pursuing exceptional sightings. Some participants still call horned owls "hootie owls"; others insist that vultures are "buzzards." At one of the first count parties, an argument broke out between two old men: One had seen several thousand brant that morning, but the other insisted that brant never recovered from the eelgrass blight in the 1930s and were extinct!

One of my early companions, who was also a world-class birder, was so specialized he was interested only in birds that were new to his many counties' lists. We were using a screech-owl recording on the dike to call wrens, kinglets, chickadees, and titmice when I noticed a pair of phoebes in a pine. Without thinking, I said their name and pointed to them.

"Oh God, how did I miss seeing them?" the specialist exclaimed. "I don't have an Accomack phoebe!"

"There are two of them. Take one."

"May I?"

That night at the party, he reported one phoebe; I reported the other.

The reason I wanted more local people involved in our Christmas Count was to try to develop a cadre of county residents who were knowledgeable enough about nature to affect decisions on such important issues as development, water use, and waste disposal. Without rivers or reservoirs to draw on, Accomackers have no source of water but our wells. Until the U.S. Geological Survey began drilling test holes a few years back, we didn't have the least idea of the quantity or quality of water we were tapping.

Although no supervisor or county administrator attends the Wachapreague count on a regular basis, it has attracted a number of youngsters who've grown into positions of community leadership. Jim Szablewicz, for example, first came to the Christmas Count as a high schooler.

He later took my course in conservation history at Yale. He's now Barbara's and my attorney.

After Jim Bruce stopped coming to the count—it's a long drive from Ohio—I did the compiling. Barbara and Anne Corson shared the cooking, feeding, and fee-collecting chores. This sometimes left us with little time to participate. During some counts, I was so busy ferrying parties to and from Cedar Island and worrying about getting all the reports right—including the occasional (and dreaded) rare-bird sightings—that I never got out to look for the woodcock or bittern that I knew was there but others had missed.

It wasn't the work alone I minded. As the count became more popular, it evolved into something different. For the first half-dozen years, I scheduled the count on the first Sunday of the Christmas period. Gradually, however, since the majority preferred it, the first Saturday of the count period became the usual day. The difference is that hunting is prohibited on Sundays in Virginia, and during those early years, I'd invite friends for the weekend who were both hunters and birders like myself. We'd shoot quail or ducks on Saturday and be up early to listen for owls on Sunday. I thought that such "total experiences" suited Frank Chapman's original concept better than the hit-and-run approach of most counts, for Chapman himself was a hunter as well as a birder. He not only wrote the first field guide for beginners (*Handbook of Birds of Eastern North America*, 1893) he also visited Virginia's Eastern Shore to collect birds for the first museum diorama seen on this side of the Atlantic.

Of all my guests who enjoyed those early Christmas Bird Count weekends, none was a better exemplar of the Chapman tradition than Ned Smith. Ned had only a high school diploma, but he was frequently consulted by university professors and museum curators for his extraordinary knowledge of nature. Ned was a competent writer, photographer, and wildlife illustrator.[*] He was also a first-class shot and a world-class birder. One of my favorite Christmas Count memories was the day Ned, conservation administrator John Gottschalk, and I encountered another birding party looking for shorebirds on the mudflats south of Wachapreague. We spied a mixed flock, and almost immediately, everyone began competing to name species. The frenzy soon died down, and some birders began to leave. Ned spoke for the first time: "There's a western sandpiper on the channel side of the semipalmates."

"I've already given the semipalmate sandpipers the once-over," a self-appointed expert remarked. "There's nothing else there."

Ned didn't take his eyes from his binoculars. "The bird closest to the water is a western sandpiper."

The expert received this as a challenge to his authority. "I'll get the guidebook and show you," he said.

When he returned, marching purposefully down the dock, Ned—again without taking his eyes from his binoculars—asked, "Is that the Peterson guide or the Golden?"

---

[*] He did the painting used on this book's dust jacket in 1981. Ned wouldn't take any money for the job, but he did accept a pair of Zeiss binoculars as a gift.

"Golden."

"Then look on page 124. The two species are compared at the bottom. Note the western sandpiper's bill droops at the tip."

There was a long silence. "Well, I'll be damned," the expert said and retreated up the dock.

Today, along with many of the thrushes, tanagers, vireos, redstarts, and warblers he once mimicked so well in our spring woods, Ned is gone. Long before most conservationists even knew the meaning of the phrase "neotropical birds," Ned used to make jokes about these species' decline to make the sorrow of it more bearable. He suggested turning threatened songbirds into "gamebirds" to encourage sportsmen to rally and restore their numbers the way we'd restored the wild turkey. He also suggested that since the only birds with expanding ranges in the world are those exotic to lands where they've been introduced, we could reverse the decline of New World birds by introducing them to the Old.

Ned liked coming here in the spring, when he could chug poppers for bluefish and help Barbara and me identify wildflowers. What I most remember about those visits was his amazing ability to call birds. One weekend, outdoor writer Lefty Kreh was also visiting and mentioned that he'd love to get a good close-up photograph of a singing cock quail. Ned took him out by the cemetery, sat him next to a clump of forsythia, and told him that the bird would land at a particular point just ten feet away. Ned then got into cover.

"Are you ready, Lefty?" he asked.

"I suppose so," came the skeptical reply.

"You've got everything set?"

"I think so."

"Okay?"

"Okay!"

Ned called. The cock quail came so fast that Lefty froze. The bird and the man stared at one another an instant before the bird whirled away.

"Do it again, Ned! I'll be ready this time! Do it again!"

Ned moved Lefty a few dozen yards and went through the same routine.

"Are you ready?"

"Yes!"

"Sure?"

"Sure!"

This time the bird was warier. A long minute passed. Lefty glanced at Ned; the quail flew in, lit, and took off before Lefty could trigger the shutter.

"Oh God, I missed it! Can you do it again, Ned? Please, Ned, can you do it again?"

But we'd run out of quail that morning, so I consoled Lefty and amused Ned by running them to a photo blind on Club House Marsh just inside Wachapreague Inlet, where they took pictures of snowy egrets, tricolored herms, little blue herons, and glossy ibis with their eggs and young. It's melancholy to recall those days now, for both the blind and the thicket on Club House Marsh are gone, long since swept away by winds and tide. And the bird count has never been the same without Ned.

CHAPTER 13

Real
Conservation

I n 1984, I sold forty acres of mature loblolly pine to pay
for more land adjoining the core farm. Selling timber
to cover an urgent expense is an old country custom. I
was, therefore, surprised when a friend in Washington
said that he hoped word of what I'd done didn't reach my
critics.

"Why not?" I asked.

"They'll make you out to be a hypocrite."

"How?"

"You're opposed to the destruction of rain forests?"

"Yes," I said.

"How can you be against that and then cut down your own woods?"

Some people are either unable or unwilling to distinguish between the permanent elimination of an ecosystem and the sustained-yield harvest of a woods that is still there after cutting, only a century younger. The reason may be that almost everyone today senses that the old equilibrium between continuity and change has been broken. Up until two decades ago, Americans were famous as boosters of change because it meant an improved standard of living for all of us. That's no longer true. Quite the contrary. Most members of the middle class now fear change. We increasingly cling to all perceived forms of continuity, especially nature. Yet the majority of us live apart from nature, and we're no longer familiar with the fact that nature is as much an ever-evolving blend of change and continuity as society is. Instead, increasing numbers of people make nature their primary symbol of permanence and imbue it with religious significance and fervor. This passion has led to a hierarchy of prejudicial attitudes. Anglers feel superior to hunters because anglers can release what they catch. Birders feel superior to anglers as well as hunters because birders imagine that they have no impact at all on nature. Yet we all exploit nature by merely being here. The problem is that the human biomass—and, consequently, the exploitation of nature—is growing at a pace that we can barely comprehend, much less control. Every minute of every hour, the world has 170 more people to house. Every hour of every day, the world has 10,212 more people to clothe. And every day of every week, the world has 245,093 more people to feed. Trying to preserve nature without taking into account such statistical realities is not merely a hopeless task, it gives a bad name to the only real hope we do have: *conservation.*

Although I'm the sixth or so conservation columnist in *Field & Stream*'s hundred-year history, I believe I've used more ink to explain conservation than all my predecessors combined. Up until the 1960s, most subscribers accepted the word as meaning the wise or sustainable use of renewable resources. With the advent of Earth Day, however, a growing number of people began challenging the very idea of a conservation editor at a magazine that was, as they saw it, devoted to killing wildlife. In their minds, conservation meant complete protection. It meant saving endangered species and preserving rain forests. Anyone doing anything seemingly counter to those lofty objectives became an adversary. Sadly, in drawing up their list of enemies, preservationists have alienated most of their strongest potential allies: people who also care about endangered species and rain forests but who understand that perpetuating nature is—first and foremost—hard physical labor far removed from the feel-good realm of petition signing.

Preservationists have converted conservation into a precious attitude rather than positive action. They discourage the participation of pragmatists who know that real conservation is about planting filter strips along erodible stream margins and riprapping the banks to prevent swollen currents from undercutting them. It's not about save-the-whale rallies. Real conservation is about constructing and annually maintaining waterfowl nesting boxes. It's not about sending money to organizations that make the impossible promise to restore all the waterfowl populations of North America. Real conservation is hands-on, net-gain, local habitat manipulation and species management. It's not about letting nature take its course.

Conservation is also about choices in our daily lives. It's not only about how we commute to work but whether we choose to commute at all. It's about what kind of fabrics we wear and what kind of beverage containers we buy. It's even about the kind of heating we have in our homes.

Most of our Locustville neighbors use oil or gas to heat, but we opted for wood and supplemental electricity. In the early 1970s; power from coal-fired plants was cheap and more dependable than energy from imported oil. Most dependable of all was our own firewood. High-BTU oak, cherry, and locust grow prolifically on our farm, and although wood smoke is a pollutant, the Atlantic Ocean is immediately downwind of us. Airborne pollutants are soon dispersed and broken down by plankton.

When we started, we found it difficult to find much reliable information about firewood. Magazine articles suggested that the average home (whatever that is) could be heated for an entire winter with only two or three cords of wood. Furthermore, the articles asserted, you needed only a couple of acres of woodland to supply those two or three cords in perpetuity. But where was this "average home"? What kind of wood was being burned? How rough were the winters? And what kind of magical timber management provides three cords of wood in perpetuity from only two acres of land?

Twenty years and five woodstoves later, we've learned that soapstone is expensive, but it holds warmth longer than metal and is the most aesthetically pleasing of all stove materials. We've also learned that in low-lying areas of the mid-Atlantic region, we're as concerned with dampness as with cold. Even during those rare winters when we have sustained periods of subfreezing temperatures, we have little snow to insulate us and reduce our need for firewood.

Consequently, Barbara and I feed two, sometimes three, stoves a day to keep the cold out of ten rooms (offices, halls, bathrooms, and bedrooms). We usually start in late November and taper off in late March. We use electric heat in the early fall, before the back porch is converted into a combination wood/mudroom, and again in the early spring, when we're finally fed up with breathing smoke and hauling ashes. Our midwinter utility bills are usually less than half those we pay at the peak of the summer air-conditioning season, so firewood is cost-effective. But to make those savings, we consume half a dozen cords, even in mild winters, and selectively cut and take the wood we burn off dozens of forested acres.

In 1986, a number of local residents formed the Eastern Shore Waterfowl Trust to raise money to build woodduck nesting boxes. With most duck populations at historically low levels, we wanted to do something to put birds back into the system. Although most of us had already put up a few woodduck nesting boxes on our own properties, we talked of a day when there would be over a thousand boxes on every pond and backwater in both Eastern Shore counties. The trouble was that we each had a different idea of the ideal box: its dimensions, the material it's made from, where it should be located and how high, and what devices should be used to keep predators out. When we turned to nongovernmental conservation organizations for their presumed knowledge, most of them responded by sending fund-raising solicitations and catalogs.

Ducks Unlimited (DU) had a conical plastic box to sell. In the early 1970s, I'd become leery of dark plastic as a material for nesting boxes. As Washington editor for *National Wildlife* magazine, I'd received letters from readers reporting that the plastic songbird nesting boxes we advertised killed incubating adults and eggs, especially when placed where the afternoon sun could strike them. When I took those letters to the National Wildlife Federation's vice president in charge of marketing, he told me that if I could find another product he could buy in bulk for less than 30¢ apiece and sell for over $5, he'd be happy to substitute it for the plastic birdhouse.

A decade later, a study conducted in Mississippi showed that woodduck hens and eggs were being cooked in DU's plastic nesting boxes, exactly the way chickadees and bluebirds had been broiled in the National Wildlife Federation's plastic boxes. Since woodduck embryos begin to die at 107 degrees Fahrenheit and hens are suffocated by heat exceeding 117 degrees, and since the stovelike interiors of DU boxes—even in partial shade and with additional ventilation holes drilled—commonly exceeded 120 degrees, I wanted nothing to do with them. But I had trouble persuading my fellow trust members to reject the plastic boxes on the basis of the Mississippi study. Most were loyal DU supporters, and DU insisted that its boxes were the best ever designed. Eventually, it wasn't science but economics that persuaded the others to accept wood. We could assemble a back-to-back nesting unit with a predator guard and pole for little more money than DU charged for its plastic nesting box alone.

With a grant of $5,000 from the Mellon Foundation, we persuaded a local contractor to provide a load of twelve-inch cedar boards, sixteen-foot pressure-treated posts, and all the galvanized hardware at cost. Another contractor gave us a good wholesale price on ten-foot sections of six-inch PVC pipe cut into forty-inch lengths for predator guards. We initiated an informal competition among three high school manual-training classes, which resulted in 150 boxes mounted on 75 poles. Had we known at the time that twelve-foot poles were amply high, we could have saved the trust hundreds of dollars, to say nothing of the back strain that goes with lugging those extra pounds of lumber into inaccessible wetlands.

We'd decided to mount our first boxes back-to-back because state wildlife publications at the time featured photographs of woodduck "maternity wards," where several boxes were either nailed to one pole or as many as ten boxes were hung from bars connecting two poles. As it turned out, those photographs depicted tame woodducks that had little choice but to use whatever boxes were available. We've learned over time that wild woodduck hens compete for prime reproduction areas by laying their eggs in the nests of other hens, which retaliate by doing the same. So much energy may be squandered in these territorial disputes that a good location with four nesting boxes may fledge fewer woodducks than the same area with just one box. Figuring that line of sight was the problem, we now mount only one box per pole, and always out of direct view of any other nesting box. This seems to work: In my home pond, I improved production by moving one nesting box just thirty feet so that a hen perched in the box's entrance hole can no longer see a hen perched in the entrance hole of another box across the pond.

With each passing year, the trust learns something new about raising woodducks, which I pass along in articles for *Wildfowl* magazine. Although the nonhunting public will never believe that duck hunters care about perpetuating ducks, I've developed a lively correspondence with readers from Oregon to Maine who've established their own waterfowl trusts and have added thousands of woodducks to the continental flyways.

The Eastern Shore Waterfowl Trust continues to experiment with different building materials (we currently prefer bald cypress for the boxes) and a variety of designs (we now favor boxes that open from the side with no exposed hardware). The U.S. Fish and Wildlife Service continues to recommend top-opening designs, but that's because biologists find it easier to catch brooding hens for banding in top-opening boxes. Since we're more interested in ducks than data, we opt for the easier access and simpler maintenance of side-opening boxes.

About five years ago, Virginia hired its first waterfowl biologist. Gary Costanzo has since guided the trust in trying to answer a number of questions about local woodduck propagation. Do our nesting boxes represent a net gain in laying hens, or are we merely short-stopping birds that would have nested further north? What is our fledging rate? What levels of mortality do local birds suffer once they leave this area?

The answer to the last question is, disturbingly high. Only about half the hens banded in trust boxes return the following spring. Hunting mortality is the most likely cause, but since waterfowl band returns have greatly declined over the past twenty years, biologists look to other possibilities. Yet band returns may be declining not because fewer birds are being shot but because fewer banded birds are being reported. Bands are simply no longer a novelty. Hunters are also discouraged by the long delays between when they report the bands and when the government acknowledges receipt. In the case of goose collar sightings, the government doesn't respond at all.

Hunters and the government have different objectives. Most hunters want to see as many waterfowl as possible and be able to shoot a few. In contrast, the U.S. Fish and Wildlife Service tries to manage ducks so that hunters can kill all they see. Rather than abide by its treaty mandate to maintain optimum numbers of birds, the Fish and Wildlife Service bows to political pressure—real and imaginary—

and sets seasons and limits according to what it believes is the maximum possible. The result is that most hunters do kill all they see—meaning one or two ducks per outing.

The federal government deals with over-exploitation not by stopping but by studying it. That's one way bureaucrats avoid blame. Unfortunately, studies usually become substitutes for remedies. If the Eastern Shore Waterfowl Trust were a governmental agency, we'd still be studying the problem of why pipe predator guards don't work. All we really care about, however, is that they don't. It took just one encounter with a six-foot black rat snake that had climbed over or under the pipe guard and eaten every duck egg in the nesting box to convince trust volunteers that we had to find a better way to keep snakes out.

First, we tried sealing the gap between the PVC pipe and the post with insulation foam. Although this may have saved some nests, snakes still managed to get into the boxes. Worse, a few raccoons in the upper end of Accomack County learned how to climb the theoretically too-slick pipe, and we couldn't stand by and "study the problem" while those clever raccoons taught others how to do it.

Galvanized metal cones are expensive to make and a nuisance to install, but we decided that we would be wasting the trust's time and money—to say nothing of the breeding potential of the birds—unless we retrofitted every post with a cone. Because our trust is small and unprofessional, we didn't need a lengthy meeting to debate the issue or appoint an action committee, whose first task would have been to schedule another meeting. Once our officers decided, through a few informal phone calls, that we should spend that year's funds on cones to keep snakes and coons out of the nesting boxes, Accomack's best metal-worker was called and persuaded to provide the necessary cones at cost. Don Drew reduced his price further by using twenty-six-gauge galvanized metal cut from three-by-ten-foot duct stock. Three-foot cones are wide enough to deter any raccoon and all but the longest black snakes. Twenty-six gauge is heavy enough to last yet light enough to bend around the posts we had to retrofit.[*] From beginning to end, the job took just a few months. We were finished before most "action committees" would have agreed on the location of their next meeting.

Years ago, a Maryland biologist estimated that two or three woodducks are added to the flyway for each new nesting box put up. State wildlife administrators made this guesstimate official by splitting the difference and calling it 2.5 woodducks per box. Everyone felt good about the number, but was it true?

Few of our trust members see hen woodies escorting more than one or two ducklings. Some midsummer hens have none. Yet our boxes show hatching rates of up to a dozen ducklings per nest. Curious to know what input predators were having on the young birds, I asked a friend to help me trap the dike around the pond and the swamp upstream one winter. We caught twenty-one raccoons and three foxes. The following spring, my son and I fished an eel-baited trotline in the pond and caught thirty-three

---

[*] At least it's heavy enough for cones in sheltered locations. Cones in exposed areas, where the wind may stress and fracture them, should be made from sturdier stock.

snapping turtles, including one so large that its shell barely fit inside a bushel basket.

The results were remarkable. Whereas the previous
summer I had seen broods of single ducklings—when I
saw them at all—I now saw several broods with up to eight
nearly fledged youngsters. If the point of putting up woodduck boxes is to produce more woodducks, predator control is as essential as box maintenance.

Our principal nesting-box pest is the starling, which, in
some areas, destroys half the woodduck clutches. A starling
will peck holes in the woodduck eggs to kill the embryos
and then build its own nest over them. Since starlings are
extremely wary and difficult to catch in the box, the trust's
strategy has been to tolerate them until their young are
nearly fledged. Then we toss out their nests, baby birds and
all. By allowing adult starlings to invest so much energy in
their first brood, we hope that it will be too late for them
to try again. Still, we lose the potential of that nesting box
for the season, and because we don't kill the female starling, we usually see her back the following spring.
Nonetheless, we've managed to limit losses in some ponds
to just one or two nesting boxes per year.

Whenever resource agencies acknowledge the potential
problem of pests, they advise the "humane removal" or
"relocation" of the nuisance species. That's dishonest. No
sensible person would ever attempt to "humanely remove"
a feisty and frightened raccoon while standing precarious-
ly on a stepladder next to a nesting box. Even if the person
succeeded, he would be irresponsible in taking the raccoon
from a habitat with which it was familiar to an unknown

area where it would have to compete with already established raccoons.[*]

Even less likely is the scenario of someone bringing out a writhing reptile from a woodduck nesting box, where it has just eaten a clutch of near-term eggs, and carefully putting it in a sack and carrying the sack some miles away, where the snake will only eat some other birds' eggs. The reality is the snake's back is promptly broken on the post supporting the nesting box. Most field researchers accept this, but their desk-bound bosses continue to reinforce the public's Disneyesque view of nature with euphemisms like "removal" or "relocation."

A number of years ago, Christine Stevens—founder of the Animal Welfare Institute—told me she hated the word *management* because it only meant killing things. That's not all it means, of course, but why do so many people find it so hard to accept death as a more humane option than the pretense of "removal"?

Two years ago, I saw what I thought was a stray cat on the dike across the pond. I admire cats, but a study at the University of Wisconsin found that each free-ranging domestic cat kills between one hundred and one thousand birds and small mammals annually. Since an estimated one million house cats live in rural Wisconsin, this means that *in Wisconsin alone, cats kill between one hundred million and one billion birds and small mammals each year.* Multiply those numbers by all the farms and suburbs in North

---

[*] Several of my neighbors like to eat young 'coon and will take all I trap; I kill and leave the older animals in a field for vultures to scavenge.

America, and you have some idea of why hunters were once legally obligated to kill every house cat they found afield, and why any cat that appears on my farm enters a free-fire zone.

I grabbed my double-barreled shotgun, a couple of rounds of BB shot, and went out the back door on a circuitous stalk down the dike. By the time I'd worked to within seventy-five yards of the animal, I realized it was a red fox, not a cat. The fox had mesmerized several geese with its twitching tail. The geese were in deep water just beyond the fox's leap, and whenever the birds were on the brink of swimming away, the fox flicked its tail, enticing the fascinated birds to come back. Predator and potential prey were so absorbed with one other that I managed to creep within ten yards to make sure I didn't cripple the fox when I fired.

I was immensely pleased. For this overweight, middle-aged writer to crawl that close to a wild vixen required some skill as well as luck. I told a colleague about it. He attended a conservation conference the next day and told others. That night I got a call from a state official who chided me for killing the fox.

"They have their place in nature too," she reminded me.

"So do I."

"It's not the same thing," she said.

"Yes, it is," I replied. "My wife and I used to take our son to a fox den when he was a little boy to watch the young foxes play with the wings of chickens and guinea fowl. Those little foxes were as cute as could be, but I also thought of the farmer's wife who'd lost her chickens and guinea fowl. I'm tired of hearing environmentally correct rubbish about foxes preying exclusively on rodents and insects."

Two nights later, the state official called back to say that she now accepted my killing of the fox. Someone had told her that red foxes were an introduced species, originally brought to North America for the amusement of sportsmen like George Washington. I told her the red fox is a Holarctic species and was certainly in North America before the eighteenth century. Some reds may have been introduced to Virginia because the more abundant gray fox climbs trees or goes to ground sooner than the red. Nonetheless, Washington and his friends had ample sport with gray foxes, as his hunting journals reflect.[*] Regardless of species, however, I didn't need a scientific rationale for what I'd done.

The caller and I ended our conversation cordially enough, but I'm grateful that, for the time being at least, I'm still master of my own labor and land. As more people come to worship nature and reject death as a wildlife management option, more landowners will keep to themselves their need to destroy pests. Real conservation will increasingly go underground, where much of it already is.

---

[*] On April 11, 1769, George Washington brought home a gray fox he'd treed, hoping it would provide a better run the following day. The next morning, Washington released the fox, chased it "for an Hour and 45 Minutes when he treed again, after which we lost him."

CHAPTER 14

The Tour

I n addition to frequent birding groups, occasional shooting parties, and rare visitors on horseback, once or twice a year a governmental agency asks permission to show off one of its projects on our farm. In October 1993, the local state forester, Walt Pond, rounded up so many sponsors for a tour that I was relieved to see only thirty people get off the bus. It's difficult to personalize a presentation, much less keep a tour on schedule, with many more participants than that.

We started with what I call the upper field pond. Although I dug it, and the U.S. Fish and Wildlife Service enlarged it, primarily to benefit wintering waterfowl, a variety of shorebirds —particularly black-bellied plovers— feed by the hundreds each spring in the stubble or wheat-planted field surrounding the pond. The impoundment lies at the upper end of a microwatershed flowing down a ditch and through two other ponds to yet another field-and-pond complex adjoining one of Accomack's most productive seaside estuaries. After heavy rains, shorebirds and waterfowl funnel up from the mudflats on rising tides to continue feeding on invertebrates and seeds in the overflowing ponds and saturated fields.

When I first acquired the seventy-five acres encompassing this pond, the pond site was only a shallow, frequently flooded ditch overgrown with huge willows. The acre of cultivated land on both sides of the ditch was sumpy, better adapted for growing smartweed than corn or soybeans. Yet because the smartweed frequently stood in ankle-deep water, the habitat had no bobwhite quail or cottontail rabbits; and because the willows provided perches for crows in the spring and hawks in the fall, there were few songbirds or waterfowl.

I got permission from my neighbor, who shared approximately a hundred yards of the ditch downstream, to bulldoze and burn all the willows on his side of the property line as well as on mine. He was delighted to extend his lawn and even contributed $300 to the cause. I persuaded him, however, to retain a crooked old persimmon tree on his side of the line that also hangs over mine. Each fall, this persimmon attracts numerous birds and mammals, including my wife and me. We gather the soft orange fruit, squeeze out the large flat pits,[*] and eat the pulp in cakes and puddings.

On my side of the ditch, I planted a row of bald cypress seedlings that will one day grow into a stately line of trees—if, in the meantime, I can discourage whitetail bucks from using them to rub the velvet off their antlers. It's curious—and frustrating—that each fall the bucks pass up more expendable gum and pine and select one of the young bald cypress to thrash to death. Each spring, I purchase and plant a replacement tree, which gives the row an uneven but, perhaps, more natural look.

Bald cypress once flourished in the Atlantic coastal plain from Florida to New Jersey. Sometimes called the "Redwood of the East," bald cypress was so important commercially in the early nineteenth century—when the redwood was barely known—that it would be more appropriate to refer to the redwood as the "bald cypress of the West." My front door is made of bald cypress lumbered from once vast tracts that grew in coastal Carolina before the Civil War. It was rough framed into a barge and sailed with leeboards, also made of bald cypress, to Baltimore, where the barge was disassembled and its

---

[*] Even the pits may be useful. During the Civil War, Confederate soldiers boiled persimmon seeds as a substitute for coffee.

wood milled into window frames, porch railings, and anything else calling for rot and insect resistance, including exterior doors.

Some people won't plant anything that will reach maturity after they're gone. Yet what greater testimony do we have to human imagination than a grove of trees planted two hundred years ago by someone able to perceive the future through our eyes? Each spring, my son feigns exasperation when he learns that I've bought more seedlings and want him to ride the planter I've rented from the state while I tow the apparatus with my tractor. Once started, Christopher takes pride in his work—maintaining proper intervals between the seedlings, making sure that no tops are broken as he inserts the young trees down between the plow blades, and ensuring that all the roots are covered by the angled wheels he's perched over. Christopher understands that for both of us, tree planting is more than a chore; it's an exercise in immortality.

If, as philosopher Ashley Montagu once suggested, there is a hierarchy of immortality from the spiritual realm to the merely artistic (meaning fame) and physical (DNA), I'm not sure that the physical—under certain circumstances—is not the most awesome of all. While digging the upper field pond, I discovered a thumb-sized piece of tabulate coral that I sent to Charley Potter at the Smithsonian, who in turn passed it on to Raymond T. Rye II in that institution's Department of Paleobiology. Rye wrote back, describing the coral and suggesting how it may have gotten into the upper field:

Tabulate corals were exclusively colonial, and the individual corallites are generally small in diameter, and elongate, like a soda straw. The tabulae, for which the group gets its name, are partitions transverse to the long dimension of the corallite, much like floors at regular intervals in a silo. . . . These corals lived in tropical seas, attached to the bottom in clean shallow water near the shore. They tended to form small patch reefs; that is, mounds that were sometimes solitary, and sometimes clustered with other mounds. Movements of the earth's crust uplifted the former sea floor at the close of the Paleozoic Era to become part of the Appalachian mountain chain. Later, streams flowing eastward out of the Appalachians carried this fossil to the place where you found it.

Tabulate corals were most abundant between 425 and 345 million years ago. Imagine a skeleton surviving from a time before the Appalachians. Imagine that skeleton being lifted up even as the Appalachians rose to a height greater than today's Rockies. Imagine the torrents of water that must have worn down the Appalachians to their present puny size and carried the coral several hundred miles to where I found it buried less than half a mile from the ocean where the coral was born so many millions of years ago. Now that's immortality!

I used an excavator to dig the upper field pond and marveled at the quiet efficiency of the new machinery compared with the clanking dragline used to dig my first pond twenty years earlier. Still, some operators of those old machines were masters of rhythm and motion in ways that younger operators will never become at the helms of their computerized equipment. Vincent Young was such a master, and so is Ben Hawker, whose crane, he says, is perfectly pitched in the key of C. You have to be sure that your instructions to Ben are absolutely clear before he begins a project. Once he and his crane are into their repertoire of new and old (slow and unaccompanied) southern gospel, he isn't easily interrupted. Ben knows hundreds of songs by heart and has sung at folk festivals from British Columbia to little colleges tucked away in the Appalachians.

"Makes me feel good to see young people cry when I sing," says Ben. "Good music should purge the soul. I only wish I could take my crane with me. Then they'd hear something beautiful!"

Despite careful calculations, I'd underestimated maximum high water in the upper field pond. The island left for nesting birds was flooded the first spring, drowning a clutch of newly laid Canada goose eggs. I asked Ben to come in with an extension arm for his crane so that he could reach out over the water and add several buckets of clay. Two days after he finished, the goose and her gander returned to the raised island, where they eventually fledged five goslings. When I thanked Ben on behalf of the birds and for giving me even more elevation than I'd asked for, he explained that the bowl in which the pond sits provides such good acoustics, he couldn't stop until he'd worked out a new rendition of "When I Can My Title Clear."

The upper field pond is a magnet for people as well as wildlife. When I try to herd the tour across the field to the cutover, participants keep breaking off to drift back and look at the lespedeza hedge, the bluebird boxes, or the mallards that had stayed on the pond. Several dozen other mallards, along with a few blackducks, woodducks, and a pair of blue-winged teal, had flown out when the bus arrived. As we talk, and despite our numbers and the looming presence of the bus, a blackduck returns, circles the pond twice, and plops in among the mallards.

"Must be a young bird," observes Don Schwab, a biologist with the Department of Game and Inland Fisheries. Hunters in the group smile in their shared knowledge that no mature blackduck would be so naive.

A new landowner asks me to identify sericea lespedeza. I do so and suggest that it's superior to the state-recommended (and discount-priced) thumbergii VA-70 variety, which, after repeated mowings and burnings, grows too tall and dense for the liking of most quail hunters.

Schwab points out that VA-70 holds its seeds longer than most other legumes, and its tall, canelike stems form a protective canopy for wildlife during snowstorms. Since other shrubs on the farm offer equally good snow protection, I suggest that the new landowner consult the latest catalog from C. P. Daniel's Sons in Waynesboro, Georgia.

"They sell nine varieties of lespedeza, each suited to a slightly different condition and purpose. You can customize your plantings any way you like."

"But what do you recommend?" the landowner persisted.

"I like a border of low-growing sericea with scattered clumps of VA-70, clusters of Atlantic coastal panicgrass,[*] a fringe of partridge pea, and even an occasional brier patch for the rabbits."

"How about letting the border grow up in whatever volunteers?" the landowner asked.

"That's one way to save some money," I acknowledged, "but you get what you pay for."

After I dug the home pond, I let nature determine what grew there. The result was swamp maple and willow. Maple may be pretty in the fall, but it has less wildlife value than oak, black cherry, or even pine. Willow is worse. It's so prolific, it will soon overwhelm any shallow impoundment. Fortunately, it can be killed by cutting the trunks and painting the stumps with a systemic herbicide. This is best done in the fall, when the tree's sap is retreating to the roots, so the poison will go there as well. Besides, in the spring, broken willow stems may fall in the water and sprout.

There are some native trees that should be encouraged. Foremost among them is black walnut. The intrinsic value of this tree, from its delicious nuts to its cabinet-grade wood, was perceived by Virginian colonists, who began exporting it to England in 1610. As Americans pushed west, however, and saw the amazing abundance of walnut, they devalued the tree and wasted it. Due to its durability

---

[*] In order to reduce soil erosion and save the cost of yearly plowing, agriculture will eventually evolve away from annual to perennial grasses. A hybridized form of Atlantic coastal panicgrass might be a good start. It does well in sand or clay; is drought, flood, and salt resistant; and produces a long and prolific seed head.

in contact with soil, the railroads cut thousands of mature trees just for railway ties. Today, due to the value of its veneer and the unique qualities of its wood in gunstocks, a single walnut may be worth tens of thousands of dollars.

Over the years, Barbara and I have experimented with two threatened species that once characterized the American landscape: the chestnut and the elm. We took our elm seedlings from a vacant lot in Washington, D.C., and thus far, none of the survivors has rust-colored frass in its crotches or "shotgun holes" where the larvae of the elm bark beetle have emerged. Horticulturists assure us that blight-bearing beetles will eventually find our elms and infest them. There are, however, new varieties that resist Dutch elm disease,[*] and the effort to acquire and plant them should be made to keep the restoration effort going.

We got our chestnut trees from the Smithsonian Institution, which wanted to introduce experimental hybrids to as many potential terrains as possible. I suspect, however, that the hybrids we received are more Chinese than American. They more closely resemble the two Chinese chestnuts we planted in the backyard than the American chestnut saplings we used to find struggling up from stumps near my father-in-law's home in the mountains of North Carolina. Legitimate hybrids are now commercially available, but if you prefer planting a closely

---

[*] The disease is caused by the fungus *Ceratocystis ulmi* and was first noticed when it began attacking elms holding the dikes of Holland. American quarantine authorities thought that they had every avenue of entry blocked but belatedly realized the disease was coming through on beetle larvae in veneer logs rather than in the live trees they had stopped.

related native American, the chinquapin produces a sweet nut relished by wildlife. Although little more than a shrub in the East, it grows to fifty feet in the West, with a trunk diameter of two to three feet.

Barbara and I have also transplanted bayberry (alias wax myrtle) sprigs, which have grown into dense hedges swarming each fall with yellow-rumped (alias myrtle) warblers. American holly is another native that does well as a hedge, although it takes far longer to reach head height than bayberry. State forestry departments don't normally sell bayberry or holly, but they have a much greater selection of native plants today than they did twenty-five years ago. State catalogs now even feature trees and shrubs of low commercial but high wildlife value. When I think of all the effort Barbara and I put into digging and transplanting red cedars, locusts, and persimmons—the first two successfully, but the persimmon never, because of its long taproot—I can't help but envy younger people today who can order twenty-five seedlings of cedar, locust (two types), or persimmon delivered by UPS to their front door for under $30.

Another landowner on the tour asks about fescue. In the mid-Atlantic region, Kentucky fescue is the most popular lawn grass due to its heat and drought resistance. Fescue, however, may actually be harmful to wildlife. Researchers have found that it sickens domestic livestock through an associated endophyte. Furthermore, once established, fescue is like willow in requiring drastic (and expensive) steps to eradicate, since it thrives on mowing and burning.

Fescue may be purged with a combination of herbicides and plowing, although it's sometimes possible to supplant with more aggressive vegetation. I've used sericea and VA-70 lespedeza to reclaim a filter strip dominated by fescue. I first disked the grass and then hand planted the lespedeza. I nurtured the lespedeza through its first growing season, then mowed and burned the strip as usual. Within three years, the taller, deeper-rooted lespedeza had overwhelmed much of the fescue, and the diversity of wildlife using the filter strip for food, cover, and travel increased several fold.

Nonnative plants are no longer promoted by public agencies, but there are some beneficial exotics to consider, such as multiflora rose and autumn olive. Virginia's Department of Transportation (DOT) once used multiflora rose as a buffer in the median strips of divided highways. The dense brier hedges not only blocked headlight glare at night, they also prevented out-of-control cars from crossing into oncoming traffic. Inspired by the DOT example, I planted multiflora rose along the main road running through the farm. Over the years, native vines have grown up in this hedge: Virginia creeper, trumpet vine, and poison ivy. A few black cherry trees have also sprung from bird droppings. Multiflora rose, however, remains the dominant species.

In the spring, the briers are lush with sweet-smelling, tiny white roses, and on clear, moonlit nights, mockingbirds sing in the hedge until dawn. In the fall, the plant's fruit hips are a high-energy food for wintering birds. Some ornithologists believe that the mockingbird extended its traditional southern range north due to the once common use of multiflora rose as a "living fence" by dairy farmers and state highway departments. The briers not only provide better than average nesting habitat for a variety of birds but are also the best cottontail cover on the farm. Twice my highway hedges have also served their original purpose by stopping out-of-control cars from rolling into the fields. And unlike the periodic potholes dug in our marsh by cars plunging off the causeway, gouges in a multiflora rose hedge are quickly closed with new growth.

Autumn and Russian olive were once recommended by state forestry agencies as good wildlife shrubs for spoil areas. They are among the few nonlegumes that fix nitrogen in the soil by means of bacterial root nodules. Barbara and I were among the first on the Eastern Shore to plant autumn olive, and one fall, workers from the Gulfstream Nursery near Wachapreague came to strip our shrubs of their berries, propagate the seeds, and sell the autumn olive seedlings to the state.

Today, Virginia's Forestry Department pretends that autumn olive doesn't exist. This olive (no relation to true olives) is so popular with birds that its seeds and, hence, new plants are rapidly spread to areas where they're not wanted. The result is that autumn olive is now banned for sale east of Interstate 95. But since this plant is easily controlled with fire or herbicides, why not let individual landowners decide whether they want it or not?

Autumn olive berries are a favorite food of the woodduck. During the farm tour, I show my visitors several areas where I've purposely planted autumn olive seedlings so that the mature shrubs' lushly laden branches will hang down into the water. I tell the tour group that if they'd like to return late that afternoon, they'll see a spectacular flight of woodducks. The most trusting (or hungry) birds fly directly in among the overhanging branches, while the more cautious ones circle the field several times before pitching and swimming under the fruity canopy. Some evenings, I see more than a hundred ducks by the time darkness falls, and I sit and listen to dozens more coming.

Autumn olive berries are also enjoyed by people. Jim Killmon, who tended our Cashville land for many years before he died, had heard the negative propaganda about autumn olive and was understandably concerned when I planted a hedge of it along the Cashville road. Jim also thought the hedge wasted a perfectly good sliver of arable land. Within three years, however, he'd changed his mind. Each fall he called to let me know how many jars of autumn olive berries he'd canned. He said that he enjoyed turning the tables on neighbors who had given him spring fruit preserves by presenting them with jars of his mysterious "autumn jelly."

CHAPTER 15

The Larger Lessons of Nature

Not long after we moved to the Shore for good, Barbara dressed me for a Halloween party as king of the male chauvinist pigs. She made a crown of pig faces, gave me a scepter with a pig's head on top, and even fixed a curly tail for my pink paper robe. I told her that I'd wear the costume because I didn't think anybody would understand it. To be sure that they did, Barbara wrote "MCP" on a large piece of cardboard and hung it around my neck just as we entered.

It made no difference. Some thought my costume was Barbara's not-so-subtle way of advertising my over-weight. Nobody knew or cared what an MCP was. When she tried to stir up the other women, most were puzzled, and one told her, "Honey, a man's either a chauvinist or a fairy, and I'll take the chauvinist every time."

Playwright Eugene O'Neill once described the ideal woman as mother, mistress, wife, and whore. A self-employed farmer, fisherman, or freelance writer also needs a woman as secretary, accountant, and, in Barbara's case, editor and travel agent. Country people adhere to traditional gender roles because the circumstances of rural life require it. Strength and mechanical savvy are important masculine criteria, whether one is repairing an irrigation pump, changing a tractor tire, or hauling a net. Domestic skill is still the measure of a woman, whether she be a teenage baby-sitter or a matron baking cakes for the annual volunteer fire department fund-raiser.

In 1991, I wrote the foreword for Michael Furtman's *On the Wings of a North Wind* as a counterpoint to the politically correct but nonsensical theory that no human activity is either exclusively male or exclusively female. I found it ironic that just as behavioral scientists were concluding that a number of highly evolved species such as the chimpanzee, African hunting dog, and bottlenose dolphin habitually form long-term male coalitions, PC theorists were clamoring for legislation designed to suppress this instinct in humans.

"Without, perhaps, realizing it," I wrote, "Furtman taps into the power of *mythology*, as the late religious scholar and anthropologist Joseph Campbell meant that word. The story of an innocent seeking experience with only an empathetic beast to share his journey is as old as the oldest Native American legend and as new as the *Star Wars* trilogy."

Questing, I said, is mostly a masculine enterprise. Every culture evolves legends concerning the journeys of young men—rarely young women—that are emblematic of the search for the meaning of life. Joseph Campbell taught for over thirty years at Sarah Lawrence College—first when it was exclusively a school for women, and later after it became coeducational. He found that although the underlying questions that intrigue young men are mostly about how things work and what they mean, women are more inclined to ask, "What will this do for me?"

The book's publisher received a spate of angry feminist mail. One letter came from a graduate student at the Delta Waterfowl and Wetlands Research Station in Manitoba. "You buy right into Campbell's idea," she wrote, "that women are interested in only the here and now, and don't care for contemplating deeper questions. As a woman scientist, I beg to differ."

Yet what "deeper question" is there than that concerning the perpetuation of our species and culture? Once a month during the prime of their lives, women are dramatically reminded of their childbearing potential and the fact they have only a relatively limited time in which to attract a suitable mate and produce offspring. By contrast, from puberty to old age, men are daily aware of our potential to produce thousands of young. A few eastern potentates have even allegedly succeeded. The reproductive strategy of women is necessarily more selective than that of men. It is in each woman's interest and, therefore, our species' interest that women unconsciously but continually ask the question, "What will this do for me?"

"As a woman scientist"—particularly an aspiring ornithologist—the Delta student must have seen female starlings in the spring sitting on overhead wires, drooping their wings, trembling like nestlings, begging for food. Male starlings respond by flying off to find sufficient food to impress the female. It's important that each male control sufficient territory, meaning resources, to be able to satisfy the begging bird he courts. Once the pair-bond is established, the male continues to demonstrate his resourcefulness by finding ample nesting material. We may smile at male starlings as the avian equivalent of Dagwood Bumstead or Archie Bunker, but our smiles are rooted in an awareness that the starlings' behavior—and our own in this regard—is perfectly normal, indeed, essential.

"As a woman scientist"—particularly one working at the Delta Research Station—my feminist critic has surely witnessed the nuptial flights of waterfowl. Half a century ago, H. Albert Hochbaum, in his monograph *The Canvasback on a Prairie Marsh,* observed that "the courtship pursuit-flights of the Mallard, Gadwall, Baldpate, Shoveller and Pintail are of unbelievable grace. I can recall no marsh scene more moving than a party of Gadwalls or Pintails high in air in the evening twilight, each drake attempting to outmaneuver the others, and the hen outmaneuvering them all."

The key to understanding the birds' behavior lies in the words "the hen outmaneuvering them all." For thousands of years, our species has observed that almost every other creature we rely on for food or companionship has mating rituals similar to our own. Males must display resourcefulness, in the most literal sense of the word, while females must attract and select the most resourceful males.

A surprising number of species are even monogamous. In the case of Canada geese and otters, females must cultivate their mates' loyalty for the duration of their offspring's infancy and adolescence. Such permanent or long-term bonds ensure that the male is always on hand to help feed and protect the young, despite his natural inclination to wander off and inseminate as many receptive females as he can find.

Both sexes of monogamous birds usually share the same plumage pattern. Birds whose sexes look very different generally take new partners each spring. Drake mallards, for example, are more flamboyant than their cryptically colored hens. Although some ornithologists categorize mallards and blackducks as the same species, the scientists are considering only genes, not behavior. The reproductive strategies of the two birds are quite different. Whereas blackduck drakes guard hens whose eggs they've fertilized, mallard drakes abandon their hens soon after copulation to look for other hens.

So long as the Atlantic and Gulf coasts of the United States were wild and undisturbed, monogamy worked to the advantage of the blackduck and its nonmigratory southern cousins: the mottled Mexicans, and Florida ducks. With the ongoing disruption and alteration of coastal ecosystems, however, the blackduck's investment in permanent pair-bonds has become a liability, and the promiscuous mallard has taken over in many areas once dominated by blackducks.

My neighbors might see a moral in this, or at least a parallel between their own monogamous lives and that of the blackduck, and contrast it with the more licentious behavior of mallards and many celebrities. Back when a majority of Americans lived on the land and honored—if not always adhered to—the principle of monogamy, our culture seemed to be as coherent as nature appeared harmonious. Now, however, the mallard side of our psyche seems to dominate, and profligacy is society's norm.

In a recent book *Adolescence and Youth in Early Modern England,* researcher Ilana Krausman Ben-Amos found that between 1550 and 1700, the mean age of marriage for men was never less than twenty-seven and sometimes as high as twenty-nine, while that for women was around twenty-six. Although no effective means of contraception was available, the rate of illegitimate births was very low, an average of no more than three percent. Premarital conceptions may have been high—throughout the period as many as one-fifth of all brides were pregnant when they got married—but that only indicates engaged couples expected to pay the consequences of premartial sex.

How did young people back then manage to restrain themselves sexually? A French historian suggests that masturbation was more acceptable in Europe before the advent of Victorianism, but Ben-Amos believes the answer lies in the fact that under the apprentice system prevalent in the centuries she studied, most young men and women worked long and hard from their early teens on. They became self-reliant and responsible in ways unimaginable to modern teenagers and their parents. In addition, the Church persuaded most young men to wait until they could afford to get married and most young women to wait until they found someone with sufficient resources to provide security for themselves and their offspring.

Scientists pooh-pooh moralistic interpretations of nature, but morality has been part of our consciousness longer than science has. Our cultural ancestors, from Aesop to Milton, believed that all aspects of nature were created for some moral lesson or purpose. Children and most adults still see nature that way, and by refusing to accept nature as a moral force in most people's lives, biologists fail to persuade the majority that science is superior to sentiment when confronting nature. The consequence of this failure is enormous, for it includes a reluctance on the average person's part to accept not only the interrelatedness of life but the inevitability of death.

Most years, the seven pecan trees in our front yard are uncertain nut producers. One tree may grow many pecans, while those on either side grow few or none. Once a decade, however, production is synchronized so that every tree in the grove has a bumper yield. When that happens, gray squirrels appear from everywhere. The ripening nuts must give off a windborne odor, or possibly the rodents are drawn to the grove by the mobs of crows squabbling in the trees.

Some people are surprised to learn that crows eat pecans. Yet both common and fish crows love the sweet nuts, and mixed flocks of both species have the capacity—as the squirrels do—to strip every last nut from the trees before we get one. That's why, when I hear a flock of crows in the grove, I sneak out the back door with a shotgun and stand close to the lilac hedge. Well-fed crows are always eager for a fight, and after just one or two caws—sometimes with my throat, but more often with a call—the entire mob comes charging to attack the hawk or owl they think their unknown cousin has discovered. Generally, the young birds—those most eager to prove themselves—rush in first and are killed. Occasionally, however, I shoot a flock elder. I can tell that even as it's falling, because the survivors' clamorous fury doubles in intensity.

I also shoot squirrels, both to protect the pecans and to obtain the tasty meat for one or more of Barbara's Brunswick stews. Since pecan trees are slow to shed their leaves in the fall, I start with a .20-gauge shotgun, hoping that enough number 6 or 7 1/2 shot will cut through the foliage and mortally wound the squirrel as it runs across limbs or leaps from tree to tree in its race for the all-ye-all-ye-in-free of the pine woods. By November, most leaves have fallen, and I can use my scoped .22.

When I see a squirrel planting nuts or scampering up a tree with another in pursuit, I take a break from writing, ease open the front door, and sometimes shoot the nut planter or tree scamperer from the front porch. If the day is pleasant, I go into the grove, stand next to a tree, and scrutinize every limb where I suspect a squirrel may be hiding. Sooner or later, I spy first an ear, then an eye.

It's tricky shooting, and not every squirrel falls dead. Some clutch and claw at the bark as they fall and then convulsively somersault on the ground. Others lurch at me because they lack the strength to run away. I admire their moxie even as I strike them into trembling death.

As a hunter and a Purple Heart veteran, I've seen my share of death, yet no matter how much I see, I never become inured to its mystery and sorrow. Some sentimentalists assume that hunting is an activity you give up once you've been to war. In my own case, war only confirmed what hunting taught me long ago: All complex organisms, including humans, respond to severe physical trauma in exactly the same way. The instant a bullet enters a squirrel or a person, peptide hormones are released by cells in the hypothalamus and pituitary gland. These substances, known as endorphins, immediately attach themselves to other cells responsible for the perception of pain. Endorphins have all the pharmacologic properties of opium. Even though a crippled person or squirrel may feel bewildered or frustrated in not being able to function normally, he or she won't feel pain for many minutes after severe wounding.

How do I know that wounded squirrels don't feel pain? Because I've talked with men who were dying of terrible wounds. Their perception of pain was usually the result of visual, not physical, stimuli. One mutilated man wanted reassurance that nobody else was hurt and then apologized for being a burden. He was calm until he looked down and saw that he was missing most of his lower body. Then he went into shock and died.

Shock is nature's way of "putting to sleep" all irretrievably damaged creatures, including humans. On a battlefield or in an accident, shock is the medic's greatest adversary, but it's a blessing in most cases. It's nature's humane way of ending a life that no longer has the capacity to fulfill the fundamental purpose of procreation.

This is not to say that pain doesn't exist. Pain is all too real for those suffering from it, but pain is always proportionate to one's chances of survival. Lewis Thomas, author of *The Lives of a Cell,* observed that "pain is useful for avoidance, for getting away when there's time to get away but when it is end game, and no way back, pain is likely to be turned off, and the mechanisms for this are wonderfully precise and quick."

When I was a boy, my friends and I heard about how old Eskimos were left on drifting ice floes to die. We were told the tale to make us grateful we would never be abandoned by our friends and families. What we were not taught, but which I've since learned by spending time among the Innuit, is that many of the elderly expect and want to die this way. Their deaths are a form of altruism, not social betrayal.

Likewise, seven outdoor writer colleagues I know of have taken their lives when the pain of cancer or the expense of treating a terminal disease began to devastate their families' resources. As hunters, all these men knew precisely where to shoot themselves for instantaneous death. Shooting, however, causes bloody wounds that are likely to be a horror for the loved ones who discover the dead. That's why one colleague waited until his family was away for the weekend before calling the police to tell them there was a body in the backyard. By the time the police arrived, there was. And by the time the man's family returned to town, his body had been made presentable.

In March 1994, the British Department of Health funded a long-term psychiatric study to determine why farmers and "others living in rural areas" have a suicide rate nearly twice that of urban people. This is ironic, because the suicide rate of farmers is actually lower than that of veterinarians, dentists, pharmacists, and physicians (including psychiatrists) in that order. However, statistics concerning the suicide rates of such professionals are treated almost like state secrets, which, considering the implications, they probably are.

Suicide rates for veterinarians, dentists, pharmacists, and physicians may be higher than for other categories of humanity not because these professions are more prone to depression but simply because such people have easier access to barbiturates than the rest of us. Farmers and "others living in rural areas" use firearms and gas ranges because that's what they're familiar with, and because we're forbidden to possess drugs.

Suicide is always discussed in condemnatory tones. In the case of young people—those whose body chemistry has betrayed them with a shutdown of the production of norepinephrine and serotonin, which help modulate emotions and aggression—who will never have the chance to fulfill their creative or procreative potential, suicide is a sad loss. Among the elderly, however,—among those who have already skimmed the cream of life—suicide may be a sensible option if the alternative is the humiliation of hospitalization and a consequent erosion of resources that could otherwise be bequeathed to the young.

I'm occasionally asked how—other than the obvious ways—country life differs from what Barbara and I knew in the city. My answer is best made in reference to senses. In Manhattan, tall buildings confused my perception of wind direction, so that on one corner, it might seem to be blowing from the east; on the next corner, from the west. I could always tell, however, that the wind was blowing from New Jersey when I stepped outside our apartment on West 88th Street and tasted zinc and copper ions in the air.

Because I didn't like much of what I tasted, saw, and heard in Manhattan, I shut down all but my most perfunctory receptors—those that enabled me, like most urbanites, to cope with the city but not necessarily to flourish there. Even then, I could hear the clanking of chains on most of those who passed me in corporate corridors.

By contrast, I relish the sights, sounds, and odors of the country. Spring plowing offers a sensory feast of freshly turned earth, the crying of gulls diving for grubs and worms in the tractor's wake, and trees that seem to green even as I work. I like the sweet smell of freshly filleted flounder and the sour odor of freshly cut red oak. Bird songs are not overwhelmed by traffic noise here, nor are the stars overwhelmed by city lights and smog. At night, I tell the cycles of the tide by the odor of the marsh, and the time (sometimes) by the distant call of the train.

Born-here neighbors will always regard Barbara and me as outsiders, but then much of that has to do with their being Virginians, famous for needing three people to change lightbulbs: one to do the work and two to talk about how good the old bulbs were. (If an Eastern Shoreman is present, he'll likely suggest the new bulbs won't work anyway.) Barbara and I have been told that if our son stays on the Shore, marries a local girl, has children, and those children have children, then *their* offspring may be accepted as truly born-here.

In the meanwhile, Barbara, Christopher, and I have been accepted by a more crucial committee of born-heres: the local mosquitoes. So long as Barbara and I were commuting from New York and Washington, we marveled—and despaired—at the way mosquitoes seemed to single us out for persecution while local people standing alongside us were relatively unplagued. Nowadays, it's our turn to stand next to guests from New York and Washington and feel a kind of perverse pride in how the mosquitoes prefer our friends to us. Perhaps, it's the local water we convert into distinguishing pheromones, but whatever the source, there's no doubt that people who live in one area gradually develop—for lack of a better word—an understanding with the local biting insects which exact a modest annual tithe of precious bodily fluids, but nothing like the quantities of blood that tourists and recent arrivals are forced to give up. Although I still make several trips a year, mostly on magazine assignments and mostly to other rural areas where wildlife is abundant, I know I'm going in harm's way, not only in regard to the many exotic cold viruses I'll encounter, but in the fact I represent fresh food for biting insects with whom I have no rapport.

I'm sometimes asked whether I have any regrets about moving to the country. I believe the only regrets one should have are for roads not taken, so I turn the question around and ask myself, do I have any regrets about not staying in harness on any of the fast tracks I once ran and not culminating my career as a professor, an admiral, or an ambassador?

Since I've written fifteen books and hundreds of articles that nobody else would likely have written, and since the professorial, flag officer, or ambassadorial ranks I might have held were taken by friends who did just as well, if not better, than I would have done, I'm satisfied that no road I might have taken could have been more fulfilling or more fun than the one I have. Furthermore, whereas my erstwhile colleagues who became professors, admirals, and ambassadors are all looking forward to retirement and doing something different with the remainder of their lives, I'm looking forward to doing exactly what I've done for the past quarter century over the next twenty-five years. I may collect and inventory insects rather than tag and study sharks. Or I may help salvage more sea turtles than whales and band more songbirds than gamebirds. I may write about rain forests in Southeast Asia rather than those in Latin America, or hike in Siberia rather than Tasmania. Whatever, Barbara will go on minding my money, our neighbors will go on minding our business, and I'll continue pursuing the serendipity of this freelance life.

APPENDIX

THE TECHNICAL LATIN

alder, European—*Alnus sp.*

arrow arum—*Peltandra virginica*

ash—*Fraxinus sp.*

bald cypress—*Taxodium distichum*

bass, largemouth—*Micropterus salmoides*

bayberry (wax myrtle)—*Myrica sp.*

beech—*Fagus sp.*

beetle, elm bark—*Scolytus multistriatus*

bittern, American—*Botaurus lentiginosus*

blackbird, red-winged—*Agelaius phoeniceus*

bluebird, eastern—*Sialia sialis*

bluefish—*Pomatomus saltatrix*

bluegill—*Lepomis macrochirus*

brant—*Branta bernicla*

bufflehead—*Bucephala albeola*

bunting, indigo—*Passerina cyanea*

buzzard, European/common—*Buteo buteo*

canvasback—*Aythya valisineria*

cardinal, northern—*Cardinalis cardinalis*

cat, house—*Felis catus*

cattail—*Typha sp.*

cedar, red—*Juniperus virginiana*

cherry, black—*Prunus serotina*

chestnut, American—*Castanea dentata*

chestnut, Chinese—*Castanea mollissima*

chickadee, black-capped—*Parus atricapillus*

chickadee, Carolina—*Parus carolinensis*

chimpanzee—*Pan troglodytes*

chinquapin—*Castanea pumila*

cicada killer—*Sphecius speciosus*

clover—*Trifolium sp.*

coot, American—*Fulica americana*

cordgrass, big—*Spartina cynosuroides*

cordgrass, salt marsh—*Spartina alterniflora*

cormorant, double-crested—*Phalacrocorax auritus*

crab, blue—*Callinectes sapidus*

crab, fiddler—*Uca sp.*

crappie—*Pomoxis sp.*

crayfish—*Procambarus sp.*

creeper, Virginia—*Parthenocissus quinquefolia*

croaker—*Micropogon undulatus*

crow, common/American—*Corvus brachyrhynchos*

crow, fish—*Corvus ossifragus*

deer, white-tailed—*Odocoileus virginianus*

dog, African hunting—*Lycaon pictus*

dolphin, bottlenose—*Tursiops truncatus*

dove, mourning—*Zenaida macroura*

drum, black—*Pogonias cromis*

drum, red—*Sciaenops ocellatus*

duck, American black—*Anas rubripes*

duck, mottled Mexican/Florida—*Anas fulvigula*

duck, ring-necked—*Aythya collaris*

duck, ruddy—*Oxyura jamaicensis*

eagle, bald—*Haliaeetus leucocephalus*

eagle, golden—*Aquila chrysaetos*

eel, American—*Anguilla rostrata*

egret, cattle—*Bubulcus ibis*

egret, great—*Casmerodius albus*

egret, reddish—*Egretta rufescens*

egret, snowy—*Egretta thula*

elm, American—*Ulmus americana*

fescue—*Festuca sp.*

flounder, summer—*Paralichthys dentatus*

fly, greenhead—*family Tabanidae*

fox, gray—*Urocyon cinereoargenteus*

fox, red—*Vulpes vulpes*

frog, southern leopard—*Rana pipiens sphenocephala*

gadwall—*Anas strepera*

gall bush—*Iva frutescens*

gannet, northern—*Sula bassanus*

goldeneye, common—*Bucephala clangula*

goldfinch, American—*Carduelis tristis*

goose, Canada—*Branta canadensis*

goose, greater white-fronted—*Anser albifrons*

goose, snow/blue—*Chen caerulescens*

grackle, common—*Quiscalus quiscula*

grebe, pied-billed—*Podilymbus podiceps*

gull, great black-backed—*Larus marinus*

gull, herring—*Larus argentatus*

gull, laughing—*Larus atricilla*

gum, sweet—*Liquidambar styraciflua*

hackberry—*Celtis occidentalis*

hawk, Cooper's—*Accipiter cooperii*

hawk, red-tailed—*Buteo jamaicensis*

hawk, sharp-shinned—*Accipiter striatus*

hay, salt meadow—*Spartina patens*

heron, great blue—*Ardea herodias*

heron, green-backed—*Butorides striatus*

heron, little blue—*Egretta caerulea*

heron, night—*Nycticorax sp.*

heron, tricolored (Louisiana heron)—*Egretta tricolor*

hickory—*Carya sp.*

holly, American—*Ilex opaca*

ibis, glossy—*Plegadis falcinellus*

jay, blue—*Cyanocitta cristata*

kestrel, American—*Falco sparverius*

kingbird, eastern—*Tyrannus tyrannus*

kingfisher, belted—*Ceryle alcyon*

kinglet, golden-crowned—*Regulus satrapa*

kinglet, ruby-crowned—*Regulus calendula*

king snake, eastern—*Lampropeltis getulus getulus*

lilac, common—*Syringa vulgaris*

locust, black—*Robinia pseudoacacia*

loon, common—*Gavia immer*

mallard—*Anas platyrhynchos*

maple, swamp—*Acer sp.*

martin, purple—*Progne subis*

merganser, hooded—*Lophodytes cucullatus*

millet—*Panicum sp.*

minnow, sheepshead—*Cyprinodon variegatus*

mockingbird, northern—*Mimus polyglottos*

mosquito—*family Culicidae*

mosquito fish—*Heterandria formosa*

mouse, field, deer, or white-footed—*Peromyscus sp.*

mummichog—*Fundulus sp.*

muskrat—*Ondatra zibethica*

needlerush, black—*Juncus roemerianus*

nuthatch, brown-headed—*Sitta pusilla*

oak, red—*Quercus rubra*

oak, swamp chestnut—*Quercus michauxii*

olive, autumn—*Elaeagnus umbellata*

olive, Russian—*Elaeagnus angustifolia*

opossum, Virginia—*Didelphis marsupialis*

osprey—*Pandion haliaetus*

otter, river—*Lutra canadensis*

owl, eastern screech—*Otus asio*

owl, great horned—*Bubo virginianus*

panicgrass, Atlantic coastal—*Panicum sp.*

partridge pea—*Cassia fasciculata*

pecan—*Carya illinoensis*

perch, white—*Morone americana*

persimmon, American—*Diospyros virginiana*

pheasant, ring-necked/Japanese green—*Phasianus colchicus*

phoebe, eastern—*Sayornis phoebe*

pickerelweed—*Pontederia cordata*

pine, loblolly—*Pinus taeda*

pintail, northern—*Anas acuta*

plover, black-bellied—*Pluvialis squatarola*

poison ivy—*Rhus radicans*

pupfish—*Cyprinodon sp.*

quail, northern bobwhite—*Colinus virginianus*

rabbit, cottontail—*Sylvilagus floridanus*

raccoon—*Procyon lotor*

rail, black—*Laterallus jamaicensis*

rail, clapper—*Rallus longirostris*

rail, sora—*Porzana carolina*

rat, Norway—*Rattus norvegicus*

redhead—*Aythya americana*

rose, multiflora—*Rosa multiflora*

rush, threesquare—*Scirpus sp.*

salamander, spotted—*Ambystoma maculatum*

saltwort—*Salicornia virginica*

sand eel—*Ammodytes americanus*

sandpiper, semipalmated—*Calidris pusilla*

sandpiper, western—*Calidris mauri*

saltwort—*Salicornia virginica*

scaup, greater—*Aythya marila*

scaup, lesser—*Aythya affinis*

shearwater, Audubon's—*Puffinus lherminieri*

shearwater, Cory's—*Calonectris diomedea*

shearwater, greater—*Puffinus gravis*

shoveler, northern—*Anas clypeata*

silversides—*Menidia sp.*

skimmer, black—*Rynchops niger*

skink, broad-headed—*Eumeces taticeps*

smartweed—*Polygonum sp.*

smartweed, dock-leaved—*Polygonum lapathifolium*

snake, black rat—*Elaphe obsoleta obsoleta*

snake, northern water—*Natrix sipedon sipedon*

spot—*Leiostomus xanthurus*

squirrel, gray—Sciurus carolinensis

starling, European—*Sturnus vulgaris*

storm-petrel, Leach's—*Oceanodroma leucorhoa*

storm-petrel, Wilson's—*Oceanites oceanicus*

sunfish, black-banded—*Enneacanthus chaetodon*

sunfish, pygmy—*Elassoma sp.*

swallow, tree—*Tachycineta bicolor*

swan, tundra—*Cygnus columbianus*

swift, chimney—*Chaetura pelagica*

sycamore—*Platanus sp.*

teal, blue-winged—*Anas discors*

teal, green-winged—*Anas crecca*

tern, Caspian—*Sterna caspia*

tern, sandwich—*Sterna sandvicensis*

terrapin, diamondback—*Malaclemys terrapin terrapin*

thrasher, brown—*Toxostoma rufum*

titmouse, tufted—*Parus bicolor*

toad, American—*Bufo americanus*

toad, Fowler's—*Bufo woodhousei Fowleri*

tuna, bluefin—*Thunnus thynnus*

turkey, wild—*Meleagris gallopavo*

turtle, eastern box—*Terrapene carolina carolina*

turtle, pond (painters)—*Chrysemys sp.*

turtle, snapping—*Chelydra serpentina*

vine, trumpet (trumpet creeper)—*Campsis radicans*

vulture, black—*Coragyps atratus*

vulture, turkey—Cathartes aura

walnut, black—Juglans nigra

warbler, yellow-rumped (myrtle warbler)—

   Dendroica coronata

weasel, long-tailed—Mustela frenata

whistling duck, black-bellied—Dendrocygna autumnalis

wigeon, American—Anas americana

wigeon, Eurasian—Anas penelope

willow, black—Salix nigra